Collins
English
GCSE
Literature

# Exam Preparation

## Support Pack

GW01465997

John Mannion

the route to Exam success for
**AQA, Specification A**

Published by HarperCollins*Publishers* Limited
77–85 Fulham Palace Road
Hammersmith
London W6 8JB

www.**Collins**Education.com
Online support for schools and colleges

© HarperCollins*Publishers* 2003

First published 2003

ISBN 000 710954 7

10  9  8  7  6  5  4  3  2

British Library Cataloguing in Publication Data

A catalogue record copy for this publication is available from
the British Library

Internal design: Ken Vail Graphic Design, Cambridge
Cover design: Barking Dog Art
Commissioning editor: Isabelle Zahar
Project management: Kim Richardson
Edited by Kim Richardson
Production: Katie Morris
Printed and bound by Martins the Printers, Berwick on Tweed

The publishers would like to thank Venessa Shakespeare for
her valuable input.

### Acknowledgements

The publishers gratefully acknowledge the following for
permission to reproduce copyright material. Every effort has
been made to trace copyright holders, but in some cases this
has proved impossible. The publishers would be happy to hear
from any copyright holder that has not been acknowledged.

Extracts from *To Kill a Mocking Bird* by Harper Lee, published
by Arrow Books Ltd, an imprint of Random House Group Ltd.
Map of Maycomb from Monroe Museum, Monroeville, Alabama.
Extracts from *A Kestrel for a Knave* by Barry Hines (Michael
Joseph, 1968) copyright © Barry Hines, 1968. Reprinted by
permission of Penguin Books Ltd.
Extracts from *Of Mice and Men* by John Steinbeck, published by
Arrow Books Ltd, an imprint of Random House Group Ltd.
Extracts from *The Lord of the Flies* by William Golding,
published by Faber and Faber Ltd.
The Guardian Newspaper for the article *Branded for Life* by
Raekha Prasad, *The Guardian* October 2, 2002.
Samaritans for the material on page 98.

# Contents

p176 ⇨  indicates a cross reference to page 176 of the Student's Book.

# Introduction

This Support Pack for Collins *GCSE English & Literature Exam Preparation* has two main purposes. The first is to provide back-up material for both students and teachers who are working with the Student's Book. The second is to add to the material in the Student's Book, which is devoted entirely to the poetry sections of the English and English Literature exams; thus it provides coverage also of the prose selections that are the focus of Section A of the English Literature exam, as well as the reading response to non-fiction/media texts and the writing questions which are included in the English exam.

## Revision sheets for poetry

Many of the revision sheets in the Teacher's Support Pack consist of concise but detailed notes on the poems that are the focus of study in the Student's Book. The notes cover the following areas: 'Setting and context', 'Form and techniques', 'Theme and interpretation' and 'Good matches' – the last listing other poems with which the poem in question may usefully be compared in the exam essay. The revision sheets not only provide an overview of each poem for the teacher, as the notes address the same issues and questions as the Student's Book, but also collectively provide an extremely useful resource for the students when they come to revise the poems for the exam.

## Additional 'Boost your grade' material

The Support Pack also includes several 'Boost your grade' revision sheets. These reproduce many of the essays that the students are asked to assess in the Student's Book, and supply the teacher with further examples of how the essays meet the criteria of their allocated grade, as well as how they could be improved to meet the criteria of the next grade up. Once students have completed their own assessment of the essays in the Student's Book they may wish to keep a copy of these sheets to remind them of the importance of meeting the examiner's criteria. The essays have not been marked comprehensively; however, the assessments given will provoke debate and enable students to engage with the criteria and their implications. Finally, the emphasis in the Support Pack, as in the Student's Book, is on pushing the student from D to C grade, and from B to A, although examples of C to B grade and A to A* have also been included.

## Revision sheets for post–1914 novels

A third major section of the Support Pack provides revision sheets for the post-1914 novels that most students choose to write on as part of their English Literature exam – *Of Mice and Men*, *A Kestrel for a Knave*, *To Kill a Mockingbird* and *The Lord of the Flies*. These are divided into the following sections: 'Setting and background', 'Plot', 'Symbols', 'Themes', 'Characters' and 'Language and style'. They are intended as a useful resource both for the teacher when preparing their lessons and for the student when revising for the exam.

## Material on non–fiction and writing

The final two sections of the Support Pack provide questions and background for students preparing for Paper 1 Section A of the English exam (Reading response to non-fiction/media texts) and for Section B of both Paper 1 and Paper 2 (questions testing writing).

John Mannion

## Nothing's Changed – Tatamkhulu Afrika

A journey back to old haunts provokes disappointment and anger.

### Setting and context

- Located in a specific place: District Six, Cape Town, South Africa.
- Set at a specific time after the end of Apartheid.
- It is necessary to know something about this place and time to fully appreciate the poem.

### Form and techniques

- Free verse. Six 8-line stanzas but the 4th stanza is divided into 2 unequal parts (like South Africa?). These lines are the key to the poem.
- First 2 stanzas are descriptive with a flowing rhythm. This breaks up as the speaker gets angrier in stanza 3.
- Contrast between hard and soft things in stanza 1. Weeds are personified.
- List in stanza 2 ends strikingly with an emotion – anger.
- 'It squats' (line 19) is one of the shortest and most emphatic lines in the poem. 'Squats' implies both ugliness and illegal occupation.
- Another emphatic short line is 'Hands burn' (line 45) which symbolises the heat of the speaker's emotions.
- Most lines are end-stopped, but occasionally the feeling overflows onto the next line (e.g. lines 15–16, 29–30 and 36–7).
- Repetition of 'and' with parts of the speaker's body emphasises the wholeness of his feeling for the place.
- Glass is used to symbolise separation. The speaker presses his nose against it, leaves a small 'O' on it and longs to break it.
- Contrast between 'haute cuisine' and 'bunny chows'.

### Theme and interpretation

- The isolated 2 lines in stanza 4 are a key section of the poem: 'No sign says it is;/but we know where we belong.' In the old South Africa there were signs saying 'Whites only', but now money rather than the law separates white and black.
- The title of 'Nothing's Changed' is ironic. District Six has completely disappeared but the attitudes that destroyed it are still there.

### Good matches

- What Were They Like?, Limbo, Island Man (past and present)
- Limbo, Two Scavengers in a Truck, Vultures (use of contrast)

## Limbo – Edward Kamau Brathwaite

A joyous limbo dance is a reminder of the dark past.

### Setting and context

- The poem works in 2 time periods – the present of the dance and the past of the slave ships that brought Africans to the Americas.
- A 3rd context is provided by the word 'Limbo' which is a sort of 'in between' place in Christian belief.

### Form and techniques

- Free verse, highly rhythmical to reflect the limbo dance described: 'limbo/limbo like me' used as a refrain.
- Very compact expression, e.g. 'stick hit sound'.
- The limbo bar is compared to 'the dark deck' of the ship – alliteration makes this image more emphatic.
- Lines that consist of single words like 'up' or 'down' are very emphatic.
- The 'down' part of the dance represents the descent into the slave ships. The drumsticks of the dance become the whips of the slavers.
- The 'up' part of the dance represents survival. This is aided by the drummers and their music: 'and the music is saving me'.
- The successful negotiation of the middle passage is followed by a 'hot/slow/step/on the burning ground', as is successfully passing under the bar in a limbo dance.

### Theme and interpretation

- The poem is a representation on the page of a limbo dance, as well as a representation of the 'middle passage' from Africa to America as slaves.
- The fact that such a terrible event can be saved, or transformed, by music is a cause for optimism.

### Good matches

- What Were They Like?, Nothing's Changed, Island Man (past and present)
- Two Scavengers in a Truck, Vultures, Nothing's Changed (use of contrast)

# Poems from different cultures and traditions

## Blessing – Imtiaz Dharker

A break in a water pipe brings unexpected joy.

### Setting and context

- No country is specified, though the details imply a developing country. It is hot.
- 'Municipal' piped water and the number of people suggest a shanty town.

### Form and techniques

- Mostly free verse, with occasional rhymes.
- The first 2 lines define the normal conditions. Extra emphasis is achieved by placing 'never' in front of the verb.
- Onomatopoeic effect is achieved in stanza 2 by using monosyllables.
- The mood changes when the pipe bursts, shown by the flowing verse (e.g. in the alliteration of 'the flow has found'), the occasional rhyme and the length of the stanza.
- Water is associated with wealth – 'rush of fortune' and 'silver'.
- The frantic scramble for water is shown by a list of increasingly desperate vessels.
- Children are transformed: 'highlights polished to perfection' as they play in the 'liquid sun' – water and light are pleasingly combined in these images.
- Religious imagery is used from the title onwards: 'a kindly god', 'congregation', 'a roar of tongues', 'the blessing sings' – this indicates the importance of water in this setting.

### Theme and interpretation

- The sudden appearance of water brings 'riches' and an almost religious joy.
- The developing world setting is not described in detail but can be inferred from the reaction to the burst pipe.
- The poem does not comment explicitly on the situation except to express joy.
- However, there is an implicit comment on the poverty that provokes such a reaction.

### Good matches

- Night of the Scorpion, What Were They Like? (insight into other countries)
- Two Scavengers in a Truck, Nothing's Changed (wealth and poverty)

## Island Man – Grace Nichols

A man who has lived in England for a long time still wakes up to the sound of the sea.

### Setting and context

- The poem is dedicated to, and inspired by, a specific person.
- It is a simple contrast between life in London and in the Caribbean.

### Form and techniques

- Free verse, with varied line lengths used to create the rhythm, and some rhyme.
- Stanzas 1 and 2 describe the man imagining he is waking on a Caribbean island.
- The sound of the surf is reflected in the irregular rhythm. Alliteration of 's' suggests the hiss of the sea on sand. Line 5 is onomatopoeic.
- The vigour and strength of the sun is emphasised by personification.
- The break in the island man's consciousness and return to London life is shown by the break in line 11.
- 'Emerald isle' image indicates the preciousness of the place, rather than a comparison with Ireland.
- Repetition of 'comes back' and 'groggily' emphasises his struggle against returning to the reality of London.
- London is not a jewel – it is 'grey', 'metallic' and 'dull'.
- London sounds are 'muffling' the sounds of the Caribbean – repetition emphasises this.
- Only his 'crumpled pillow' is left to remind him of the waves he has left.
- The final line is isolated. It is a return to normal but it is cut off from the man's inner life.

### Theme and interpretation

- The poem contrasts two different atmospheres: the brightly lit Caribbean full of human and natural activity, and dull, grey, mechanical London.
- The poem is dedicated to one individual but it reflects a common experience for people who have made a major change in where they live.

### Good matches

- Two Scavengers in a Truck, Nothing's Changed (two cultures)
- Vultures, Limbo (contrasting views)

GCSE English & Literature: Exam Preparation Support Pack © HarperCollins *Publishers* 2003

# Poems from different cultures and traditions

## Night of the Scorpion – Nissim Ezekiel

A woman is stung by a scorpion – the neighbours gather to offer support and advice.

### Setting and context

- This poem seems to be autobiographical.
- The details of the poem – lack of electric light, neighbours described as peasants – suggest a rural setting in a developing country.

### Form and techniques

- Free verse. One long stanza and one very short stanza. The final stanza is a comment from the mother.
- The scorpion is described as 'diabolic' (line 6) which introduces the idea of evil to the poem.
- Extended image used to show that the neighbours are pests: they come 'like swarms of flies' and 'buzz' their ideas and opinions. Their shadows are like 'scorpions'. Repetition in lines 32–3 reinforces this.
- Repetition of 'they said' undermines the neighbours' comments, as it implies all of them are making the different comments.
- Mother's suffering is emphasised by alliteration and assonance in lines 34–5 and 41.
- The simple and brief lines 44 and 45 conclude the episode with an air of anti-climax – or exhaustion?

### Theme and interpretation

- The poem expresses irritation at people who prefer to sit and comment on another's pain and suffering instead of doing something about it.
- The father is faintly ridiculous but at least he is active.
- The final comment is left to the mother. She has endured pain throughout the poem and so her final remark is genuinely generous and caring.

### Good matches

- Two Scavengers in a Truck, Nothing's Changed (two cultures)
- Vultures, Limbo (contrasting views)

## Two Scavengers in a Truck – Lawrence Ferlinghetti

A snapshot contrasting rich and poor in America.

### Setting and context

- This poem is set in a particular time and place – 9 a.m. in downtown San Francisco.
- However, it seems to be making a broad statement about rich and poor in America.

### Form and techniques

- Free verse. Line length and page layout are used to control how the poem is read.
- The language is as informal as the layout.
- The poem is very American in its perspective and in its choice of language, e.g. stoplight, downtown, garbage truck, stoop, hip, grungy, cool, odorless.
- The title refers to the garbagemen as 'scavengers' as if they were dependent on the garbage they collected rather than their wages.
- The 'beautiful people' are beautiful not because of their looks but because of their wealth and social position.
- The garbagemen look down on the beautiful people – this is the reverse of what normally happens in society and probably what caught the poet's eye.
- However, the garbagemen do not observe their own reality – they see the beautiful people as if in an 'odorless TV ad'.
- Repetition of 'as if' to indicate the possibilities of American democracy.
- Seafaring imagery used at the end – 'small gulf' and 'high seas' of American democracy – to make a political point.

### Theme and interpretation

- The poem contrasts people from either end of the social spectrum.
- It is a statement about the American Dream, which in theory means that anyone can achieve anything if they work hard.
- The garbagemen have been working hard, but the poem suggests that crossing the gulf that separates them from the rich and beautiful people will be difficult.

### Good matches

- Limbo, What Were They Like?, Vultures, Nothing's Changed (use of contrast)
- Blessing, Nothing's Changed (wealth and poverty)

## What Were They Like? – Denise Levertov

The people of Vietnam are evoked through a series of questions.

### ◗ Setting and context

- The author is an American who disapproves of her country's conduct in the Vietnam War.
- The poem is set at some future time when the people of Vietnam have disappeared from the world.

### ◗ Form and techniques

- Free verse. The 1st section consists of 6 questions; the 2nd section contains the answers to the questions.
- The questioner appears to be a sophisticated voice, perhaps a male student of history – addressed as 'Sir' in answers 1 and 3.
- The answerer is also unidentified – possibly a local (South East Asian) anthropologist or expert.
- The fact that the questions have to be asked implies that it is no longer possible to observe the people of Vietnam directly.
- The questions are put together at the start of the poem to build up suspense.
- Symbolism is used to express some ideas, e.g. 'light' meaning carefree in answer 1; 'buds' standing for children in answer 2; 'bones' meaning both jewellery and human bones in answer 4.

- Powerful metaphors include the 'mirrors' (answer 5) – paddy fields smashed by bombs.
- Delicate similes include speech/song and singing/flight of moths in moonlight in answer 6.
- Comparisons are used because the things being described are no longer in existence.

### ◗ Theme and interpretation

- Even though the people of Vietnam were not wiped out in the war, the poem suggests that a great deal of Vietnamese culture was lost.
- Poem deals with loss. Delicate and fragile things do not survive a war: instead, war consists of harsh and terrible things such as smashed mirrors or burned mouths.
- The poem consistently contrasts these 2 areas of experience.

### ◗ Good matches

- Nothing's Changed, Limbo, Island Man (past and present)
- Limbo, Two Scavengers in a Truck, Nothing's Changed (use of contrast)

## Vultures – Chinua Achebe

Two vultures roosting by a roadside prompt thoughts on the nature of evil.

### ◗ Setting and context

- The poem is set principally in the Biafran war, although this is not mentioned explicitly.
- The 2nd part of the poem explicitly refers to the Second World War.
- By implication the poem is relevant to all human conflict.

### ◗ Form and techniques

- Free verse in 3 sections separated by an ellipsis (3 dots). The 2nd section is itself in 2 parts, again separated by an ellipsis.
- A logical structure: observation, reflection, further example, general reflection.
- The stylistic structure is descriptive, reflective, descriptive, reflective.
- The opening mood is grim – 'greyness', 'drizzle', 'despondent' – also emphasised by the alliteration of 'd' in lines 2 and 3. The vultures have 'bashed-in' heads.
- Description of the vultures and corpse arouses disgust. Their affectionate gestures are a discordant note in this context.
- Reflection is introduced by the word 'strange' (line 22).
- Love is personified in lines 22–9, and contrasts with death in the 1st section.

- Shock effect of 'human roast' in line 33 – as if the victims were being cooked.
- The commandant's 'hairy nostrils' are similar to the vulures' 'gross feathers'. He is ugly but capable of love.
- Ordinary domestic images are used to suggest love, e.g. 'Daddy's return'.
- The contrast in the final section between ogre and glow-worm suggests that evil is bigger than love.
- Achebe's conclusion offers a choice of responses but is weighted in favour of despair.

### ◗ Theme and interpretation

- Achebe is interested by the fact that creatures that love can also carry out acts of great evil.
- He suggests at the end of the poem that these 2 factors may be more closely related than people like to think.

### ◗ Good matches

- What Were They Like?, Limbo, Island Man (past and present)
- Limbo, Two Scavengers in a Truck, Nothing's Changed (use of contrast)

GCSE English & Literature: Exam Preparation Support Pack © HarperCollins *Publishers* 2003

## from 'Unrelated Incidents' – Tom Leonard

An unusually forthright news broadcast in an unusual accent.

### Setting and context

- The poem consists of an ironic interpretation of a news bulletin.
- It is written in Glaswegian accent and dialect.

### Form and techniques

- Free verse. Very short lines, with 2, 3 or 4 syllables. Rapid pace.
- 'thi man said' (lines 3–4) shows that the poem is an interpretation of the news bulletin as reported by the speaker.
- The line with the largest number of syllables is 'BBC accent', which emphasises its importance.
- Non-standard spelling is used to represent the speaker's accent – the spelling is commented on by the speaker who implies that it is not as acceptable as standard English spelling.
- Capital letters are not used, as this reflects spoken rather than written language.
- Several words are run together, e.g. 'toktaboot' for 'talked about' and 'thirza' for 'there is a' – characteristic of the way people speak.
- Other words, e.g. 'widny', are recognisably Scottish in origin.
- Slang terms, e.g. 'yoo scruff', zemphasise the difference between this and a normal news bulletin.
- The poem ends on an aggressive note – 'belt up' – which is either a comment by the newsreader, who is not interested in the views of others, or a comment by the angry speaker of the poem, telling the newsreader to shut up.
- The phonetic spelling and short, simple sentences make the meaning clear despite the Glaswegian accent.
- The risk of putting readers off is outweighed by the striking and unusual effect achieved.

### Theme and interpretation

- Poem uses non-standard English to make a point about our own and the media's attitude to regional accents and dialects.
- People expect 'the truth' to be delivered in a 'BBC' (that is, non-regional) accent, and not in the everyday speech of their region.

### Good matches

- Search for My Tongue, Half-Caste (language issues/use of non-standard English)

---

## from 'Search for My Tongue' – Sujata Bhatt

A discussion of the tensions caused by speaking constantly in a foreign language.

### Setting and context

- The speaker relates how she stopped speaking Gujerati and assumed that she had 'lost' it, until it returned through dreams and other routes.
- Gujerati – one of the main languages spoken in India – is the poet's mother tongue.

### Form and techniques

- Free verse in a single stanza. Some lines are in Gujerati script which are then transliterated to help non-script readers pronounce them. An English translation follows.
- The poem starts as if part of a conversation – appropriate for a poem about speech. The 'you' is not identified.
- Poem plays on the idea of 'tongue' as both a piece of flesh in the mouth and as spoken language. The phrase 'lost my tongue' is a pun meaning 'unable to speak' and 'without access to my native speech'.
- The tongue imagery powerfully expresses the speaker's feelings, starting with the uncomfortable idea of 2 tongues and then the horrific image of 1 tongue rotting and having to be spat out.
- The 2nd set of images plays with the idea of 'taste buds'. These become the buds of a plant which grows in the mouth and finally 'blossoms'.
- The device of using Gujerati script in the middle section of the poem graphically illustrates the difference between the speaker's 2 tongues and suggests that they can co-exist in the same place.

### Theme and interpretation

- The poem explores the effect of living in a foreign country and constantly speaking a foreign tongue.
- The site of conflict for the speaker is the mouth and tongue, and this is illustrated through both the imagery and the use of Gujerati script.
- The poem ends optimistically with the idea that one's original tongue (and the identity that goes with it) is never truly destroyed.

### Good matches

- Unrelated Incidents, Half-Caste (language issues)
- Presents from My Aunts in Pakistan, Hurricane Hits England (living in a foreign country)

## Love after Love – Derek Walcott

The speaker imagines a time when you will learn to love yourself.

### ◗ Theme and interpretation

- A very personal poem, which paints an optimistic picture of life after love.
- It uses simple language and everyday situations to reflect on a common human problem.
- Its conclusion is that the past is something that should be savoured and enjoyed rather than regretted.

### ◗ Setting and context

- The setting is non-specific and could be applied to love anywhere.

### ◗ Form and techniques

- Free verse, in 4 irregular stanzas.
- The 1st stanza is in the future tense – a promise of a better future – the 2nd and 4th stanzas shift into the present tense, and the 3rd stanza refers mainly to the past.
- A positive mood is established by words like 'elation' and 'feast'.
- There is a fantasy element in the meeting of 2 aspects of the self looking back at the past – there is no bitter loneliness here.
- Imperative forms are used frequently, e.g. 'sit here', 'Eat', 'Feast' – establishes the tone of an enthusiastic host caring for a guest.
- The final instruction to 'Feast on your life' shows memories of the past should be nourishing and not a source of regret.
- There are echoes of a church service in the instructions 'Give wine', 'Give bread': the ordinary act of eating and drinking is a symbol of something much more significant.

### ◗ Good matches

- This Room, Presents from My Aunts in Pakistan, Not My Business (personal responses)
- Presents from My Aunts in Pakistan, Hurricane Hits England (past and present)

## Half-Caste – John Agard

A comment on the absurdity of the term 'half-caste'.

### ◗ Setting and context

- The poem seems to be a rebuke to someone who has thoughtlessly used the term 'half-caste'.

### ◗ Form and techniques

- Free verse in 4 stanzas. 1st and last stanzas are very short, forming an introduction and conclusion.
- There are 2 speakers. The 'half-caste' speaks first, excusing his self-description. The 2nd speaker then attacks the use of the term 'half-caste' in the rest of the poem.
- 'Explain yuself/wha yu mean/when yu say half-caste' is used as a refrain.
- Rhyme is also used for emphasis and humour.
- '/' used to mark pauses in the reading and as a sort of exclamation mark.
- 3 images are used to make the central point about mixtures: paint, light and music.
- Paint – great art, such as Picasso's, is impossible without mixing paint.
- Light – the mixture of light in the sky is a characteristic of the English weather and, by extension, of Englishness.
- Music – the great composer Tchaikovsky shows what can be achieved by the mixture of black and white keys on the piano.
- The 4th 'Explain yuself/wha yu mean' is different and therefore stands out. It leads into a satirical attack on the idea of anything human being 'half'.
- Repetition of 'de whole of yu' emphasises the poem's attack on lazy thinking and speech.

### ◗ Theme and interpretation

- The poem is about taking pride in yourself.
- The 1st section emphasises the fact that great beauty comes from mixing.
- The 2nd section ridicules the idea of describing yourself as 'half' of anything.
- The poem's praise of mixtures is also shown by its mixture of Caribbean and standard English.

### ◗ Good matches

- Search for My Tongue, Unrelated Incidents (language issues/use of non-standard English)

## This Room – Imtiaz Dharker

A happy event affects every aspect of life in a single room.

### ◼ Setting and context

- The location of the room is not specified, nor is the cause for celebration, though a ceiling fan suggests a hot country.
- The room contains a bed and cooking equipment, indicating that the speaker is not well off.

### ◼ Form and techniques

- Free verse, with irregular stanzas and some rhyme. The final stanza is an emphatic single line.
- It is unclear what is causing the disruption to the room at first, but by stanza 2 we learn that nightmares are receding and clouds are breaking up – these are happy thoughts.
- Transferred epithet on 'bed' and 'nightmares' – the occupant of the bed presumably had nightmares.
- The cause for celebration is 'improbable' – as is the behaviour of the objects in the room.
- Alliteration of 'pots' and 'pans', and 'celebration' and 'clang'. 'Clang' also rhymes with 'bang' – all of these sound effects indicate that the celebration is noisy but enjoyable – 'no one is looking for the door'.

- In stanza 4 even the speaker's body seems to be disrupted by the celebrations.
- Only in the final line does the speaker move beyond the room to join in with wider celebrations.

### ◼ Theme and interpretation

- The poem is an attempt to describe the unsettling effects of unexpected happiness.
- The disruption to the normal course of events is mirrored by the uncharacteristic behaviour of the objects in the room.
- The room's behaviour is thus an extended metaphor for happiness.

### ◼ Good matches

- Love after Love, Presents from My Aunts in Pakistan, Not My Business (personal responses)
- Presents from My Aunts in Pakistan, Not My Business (other places)

## Not My Business – Niyi Osundare

Ignoring others' problems leaves a man defenceless.

### ◼ Setting and context

- This poem closely follows a well-known statement by the German anti-Nazi activist Pastor Martin Niemöller, which begins 'First they came for the Jews and I did not speak out – because I was not a Jew.'
- It is an African version of a similar set of circumstances.

### ◼ Form and techniques

- The first 3 stanzas consist of 4 lines telling of the fate of a neighbour or acquaintance followed by a 3-line chorus.
- This pattern is broken in the final stanza but many of the things mentioned earlier reoccur, including the time of day, eating a yam and the sinister jeep.
- The repetition of the same idea 4 times emphasises the importance of the story and the need to learn from it.
- The different 4th version draws attention to the fact that even those who look on with indifference are at risk.
- The time of day for each arrest is given but these are not in chronological order – the arrests disrupt the normal order of things.

- In stanza 1 the jeep has a 'belly', as if it were a hungry animal.
- In stanza 2 'off to a lengthy absence' echoes the kind of official euphemism that might be given out after an arrest.
- Transferred epithets are used to make the final stanza more striking, e.g. 'froze my hungry hand' and 'bewildered lawn'.
- Repetition of 'waiting' and the word 'usual' in the last line imply that the sinister jeep has now become a fixed part of people's lives.

### ◼ Theme and interpretation

- The poem is a warning about the dangers of selfishness when living under oppression.
- Such warnings are often ignored and so repeated examples are provided.

### ◼ Good matches

- Love after Love, Presents from My Aunts in Pakistan, This Room (personal responses)
- Presents from My Aunts in Pakistan, This Room (other places)

# Poems from different cultures and traditions

## Presents from My Aunts in Pakistan – Moniza Alvi

A girl's aunts send her clothing from Pakistan which she likes but finds embarrassing.

### Setting and context

- The poet – and perhaps the speaker – was born in Pakistan but left when she was a very small child.

### Form and techniques

- Free verse, in irregular stanzas. Variable line length is used to indicate pauses.
- Clothes from Pakistan have exotic and beautiful colours compared with the dull English clothes.
- A disturbing note is introduced by the bangle snapping and drawing blood.
- Embarrassment is described in terms of heat: speaker is 'aflame' and cannot rise up out of the 'fire'.
- However, at other times the clothes are admired and seen as a link with the speaker's past.
- The requests by the aunts for cardigans from Marks and Spencers show how tastes differ in different communities.
- The simple verbs of the speaker compared with the politer, more complex desires of the mother and aunts ('requested', 'cherished') shows the contrast between their desires.

- The speaker's images of Pakistan are all fragments – clothes, photos, newsprint.
- A shift in perspective to life in Pakistan at the end: 'staring through fretwork' suggests her separation from that culture, and that the aunts' lives are limited.
- 'Of no fixed nationality' echoes the legal phrase 'of no fixed abode' – a strong version of homelessness.

### Theme and interpretation

- The poet uses clothing as metaphor for the Pakistani part of her life. They are beautiful and fascinating but they do not fit into the drabber life of England.
- The poem explores ideas of belonging. The speaker is torn between her 2 cultures.

### Good matches

- Hurricane Hits England, Search for My Tongue (two cultures)
- Hurricane Hits England, Love after Love (past and present)

## Hurricane Hits England – Grace Nichols

The arrival of a hurricane makes someone feel better about living in England.

### Setting and context

- This poem was written after hurricane-force winds hit the southern coast of England in 1987.
- Hurricanes are common in the Caribbean, where the poet grew up.

### Form and techniques

- Free verse, in stanzas of irregular lengths. The 1st stanza introduces the poem.
- Metaphor ('howling ship of the wind'), simile ('Like some dark ancestral spectre') and personification ('gathering rage') are used in stanza 1 to establish the wind's power.
- However, to someone used to hurricanes all of this is 'reassuring'.
- The invocations to Caribbean and West African storms or storm gods in stanza 2 establish the cultural heritage of the speaker.
- The hurricane god 'speaks' through the havoc it causes (lines 15–18).
- The oxymoron 'blinding illumination' emphasises the power of the storms.
- The uprooted trees are a metaphor for the speaker, who has also been uprooted.

- A change in mood – from puzzlement to acceptance – is signalled by the passionate cry in the 1-line stanza 6: 'O why is my heart unchained?'
- Images in the final stanza – the frozen lake broken and tree roots disturbed but not damaged – are optimistic.
- Repetition on the last line emphasises the message of the poem.

### Theme and interpretation

- The poem mixes the familiar and the unfamiliar in a positive way. The speaker is not at home in the English landscape, but a hurricane familiar to her from her home in the Caribbean reminds her that the earth is one place after all.

### Good matches

- Presents from My Aunts in Pakistan, Search for My Tongue (two cultures)
- Presents from My Aunts in Pakistan, Love after Love (past and present)

GCSE English & Literature: Exam Preparation Support Pack © HarperCollins *Publishers* 2003

# Boost your grade: from D to C

## Poems from different cultures: cluster 1

pp34–35 ⟹

This is the response to the essay question that you assessed on pages 34–35 of the Student's Book. It was awarded a grade D. The annotations on the right show why the extract was awarded a D, and how you could turn it into a grade C. Words in bold are quoted from the examiner's assessment criteria.

---

D grade: **some extended supported comment.**

To turn this into a grade C, you need to use quotations more effectively. For example:

*Ferlinghetti shows the difference between the garbage men and the couple in the Mercedes by referring to the "bright yellow" truck designed to take rubbish and comparing it with the more attractively described "elegant open" Mercedes that the "elegant" couple are in.*

This would fulfil the C grade criterion **effective supporting use of textual detail.**

---

D grade: **awareness of feeling(s), attitude(s) and ideas.**

To turn this into a grade C, you need to show more understanding of the attitudes and ideas. For example:

*Although the "peace of understanding" was in each face, the villagers could do little more than bring cards and lanterns to see better.*

This would fulfil the C grade criterion **understanding of feelings, attitudes and ideas.**

---

D grade: **comment on effect(s) achieved by writer.**

To turn this into a grade C, you need to build on this comment by suggesting the poet's *purpose* in choosing the specific vocabulary that he uses. For example:

*The writer emphasises the difference in class by presenting the garbage men as common scavengers dressed in cheap man-made "red plastic blazers", and contrasts them with the more elegantly dressed couple in the "hip ... suit".*

This would fulfil the C grade criterion **awareness of authorial techniques and purpose.**

---

In this essay, I will look at the way people are presented in the two poems, "Two Scavengers in a Truck" and "Night of the Scorpion". Both poems contain descriptions of a time and a place on which the poet is commenting. The way the people are described tells us about what the poet is trying to say about the situations – so it's important to look closely.

The "Two scavengers in a Truck" are garbage men on their way home from their "grungy" job. While they are stopped at traffic lights, they are next to a rich couple in an expensive car and the differences between the people is what Ferlinghetti writes about. "In Night of the Scorpion", the poet's mother has been stung and is in pain and might die. The poem seems to be about the way that the neighbours try to cure her of the sting. The way the villagers react to the sting is interesting because they have strong beliefs but don't really help.

The scavengers are dressed in "red plastic blazers" which sound horrible and cheap. The couple are dressed expensively. The man is wearing a "hip" three piece linen suit" and the woman is wearing "a short skirt and coloured stockings". The people in "Night of the Scorpion" are described in a different way because we do not know what they look like. We only know that the peasants were like "swarms of flies" and said a lot of prayers. This seems to say that there were not very helpful.

---

GCSE English & Literature: Exam Preparation Support Pack © HarperCollins *Publishers* 2003

This is the response to the essay question that you assessed on page 35 of the Student's Book. It was awarded a grade C. The annotations on the right show why the extract was awarded a C, and how you could turn it into a grade B. Words in bold are quoted from the examiner's assessment criteria.

---

C grade: **understanding of feelings, attitudes and ideas.**

To turn this into a grade B, you need to be more specific about what feelings, attitudes or ideas are being presented. For example:

*The poet uses people's reactions to specific events to discuss their prejudices and cultural beliefs.*

This would fulfil the B grade criterion **appreciation of feelings, attitudes and ideas.**

---

C grade: **awareness of authorial techniques and purpose.**

To turn this into a grade B, you need to explain the effect of the image, to show that you understand why the poet used it. For example:

*The writer uses the simile "like swarms of flies" and the metaphor "buzzed" to represent the gathering of the many peasants, who are as annoying and as noisy as insects.*

This would fulfil the B grade criterion **understanding of a variety of writer's techniques.**

---

C grade: **understanding of feelings, attitudes and ideas.**

To turn this into a grade B, you need to use a connective to introduce the comparison, and embed the quotation in your sentence. For example:

*Ferlinghetti focuses on the way the people look different to expose the gulf between them, whereas "more candles, more lanterns, more neighbours" reveals Ezekiel's attitude to the villagers' support for the woman.*

This would fulfil the B grade criteria **appreciation of feelings, attitudes and ideas and effective use of textual detail with integrated cross reference.**

---

I intend to compare and contrast the different ways in which people are presented in "Two Scavengers in a Truck" by Lawrence Ferlinghetti and "Night of the Scorpion" by Nissim Ezekiel. Both poets present a specific event – it is the way that the people in these events are depicted that allows the reader to understand what the poets are trying to say.

In the Ferlinghetti poem, two garbage men (described as "scavengers") are stopped at traffic lights next to a young successful couple in "an elegant open Mercedes". It is the differences between the two sets of people that seem to interest the poet. The world in which the "elegant couple" live is very different to that which the scavengers live in, although they live in the same country with the same laws. In "Night of the Scorpion", the poet's mother has been stung and is seriously ill. Ezekiel seems more interested in the belief of the people around her ("who buzzed the name of God a hundred times to paralyse the Evil One") that she can be saved by prayer.

One big difference between the two poems is that in "Two Scavengers in a Truck, Two Beautiful People in a Mercedes" the poet does not talk about what the characters do or what they might say, just what they look like, while "Night of the Scorpion" is interested in what the people in the poem believe and what they say and do. Although the poets are trying to say something about the people and what it's like to live where they do, they do it in different ways.

# Boost your grade: from B to A

## Poems from different cultures: cluster 1

This is the response to the essay question that you assessed on page 41 of the Student's Book. It was awarded a grade B. The annotations on the right show why the extract was awarded a B, and how you could turn it into a grade A. Words in bold are quoted from the examiner's assessment criteria.

I shall look at the way Edward Kamau Brathwaite and Denise Levertov use language to express their feelings about the cultures they are writing about. I will examine what they are saying about the cultures and the poetic techniques they use to do so.

In "Limbo" Kamau Brathwaite looks at the limbo dance and what it actually means. There seems to be two different things going on in the poem at once. The first is a limbo dancer performing the dance with the aid of drummers in the background who are "calling" and "praising" him while the second has more sinister undertones as it refers to the "dark deck" of slavery and recalls the passage of Africans in the slave ships on their way to the Caribbean.

The rhythm of the drums is heard in the poem which has a very strong beat due to the repetition in the mostly short lines. There is also a chorus, emphasizing the sense of performance:

limbo

limbo like me

The beat helps to visualise the dance but the words often seem to mean more than one thing. For example the "stick" can be the bar under which the dancer must pass or the stick with which the slaves would have been beaten. The fact that these words can be taken to mean such different things suggests that Brathwaite is proud of the Caribbean culture, but also aware of the wrongs that have been done to his people.

---

**B grade: appreciation of feelings, attitudes and ideas.**

To turn this into a grade A, you need to show your opinion of the strong feelings expressed in the poem. For example:

*The drummers in the background are celebrating and encouraging when they are "calling" and "praising" but these positive images are tainted by the sinister references to the "dark deck" of slavery. Here the limbo stick represents the barbaric beating, not of the drums but of the bare skin of the slaves.*

This would fulfil the A grade criterion **exploration of and empathy with writer's ideas and attitudes.**

---

**B grade: understanding of a variety of writer's techniques.**

To turn this into a grade A, you need to explain how the technique reveals strong feelings. For example:

*The strong rhythm of the drum beat is used in conjunction with the chorus to emphasise the unity of the slaves, who would have sung rhythmic songs together, like a chorus, but in order to keep their spirits up.*

This would fulfil the A grade criterion **analysis of a variety of writer's techniques.**

---

**B grade: appreciation of feelings, attitudes and ideas.**

To turn this into a grade A, you need to move from appreciation to empathy, i.e. show awareness of the effect of the wrongdoing. For example:

*Brathwaite expresses his pride about the way the slaves continually limboed under the stick, but also despairs of the fact that they had to endure the pain and suffering of the beatings represented by the stick.*

This would fulfil the A grade criterion **exploration of and empathy with writer's ideas and attitudes.**

GCSE English & Literature: Exam Preparation Support Pack © HarperCollins *Publishers* 2003

A grade: **exploration of and empathy with writer's ideas and attitudes.**

To turn this into a grade A*, you need to show how the poet's idea helps you understand what it must have been like for the slaves. For example:

*The limbo stick gets lower and lower, making it harder for the dancer to get under it, just as the slaves would have felt more and more pain as their dark journey proceeded.*

This would fulfil the A* grade criterion **consistent insight and convincing/imaginative interpretation.**

A grade: **references integrated with argument.**

To turn this into a grade A*, you need to go into more detail in your analysis of the text. For example:

*The silence becomes more threatening during the poem. At first it is "in front of me" and then it is "over me", as if it is swallowing the slaves up in the hold of the ship.*

This would fulfil the A* grade criterion **close textual analysis.**

A grade: **exploration of and empathy with writer's ideas and attitudes.**

To turn this into a grade A* you need to enhance the exploration and empathy with consistent insight. For example:

*Therefore "the music is saving me" refers to the power of music, which was used as a way of asserting their common front against the aggressors – effectively their only form of retaliation.*

This would fulfil the A* grade criterion **consistent insight and convincing/imaginative interpretation.**

This is the response to the essay question that you assessed on pages 41–42 of the Student's Book. It was awarded a grade A. The annotations on the right show why the extract was awarded an A, and how you could turn it into a grade A*. Words in bold are quoted from the examiner's assessment criteria.

In this essay, I intend to compare "Limbo" with "What Were They Like?", analysing the ways in which the poets display their feelings about the cultures they write about.

"Limbo" by Kamau Brathwaite concerns limbo dancing (as well as connotations of the word 'limbo') – considering it both as a spectacle that tourists to the Caribbean might expect to see and as a metaphor for the Middle Passage – the route via which Africans were transported as slaves to the Americas. The limbo reportedly originated on the slave ships in order to keep the "cargo" fit and healthy and is now a traditional Caribbean dance. Brathwaite's poem considers the origins of the dance at the same time as describing a modern performance. Many of the words he uses can be interpreted in different ways. For example if you look at the line "And limbo stick is the silence in front of me", it can be seen as the literal limbo stick that the dancer must go under, while the "silence" can also be read as the fear of the slaves on the ships, who were ignorant of where they were being taken or whether they would survive the voyage. Their cultures and religions had also been "silenced" by the slave trade. The "stick" might represent the bar for the dance as well as the instrument that slave traders may have used as a weapon.

"Darkness" is another major theme in the poem and is linked to the "silence". On a simple level, it may mean that the dance is taking place at night but it also refers to a people who have had their lives thrown into darkness – not just the darkness of the hold of the ship where they were stored, but also the obscuring of their history and culture (the history of the period would have been written by Europeans). Brathwaite seems to be celebrating the fact that in spite of the horrors of slavery, many of the customs have survived. Their gods had been rendered "dumb" by the transportation but the dance lifts them "out of the dark". This is both the dancer rising up having gone under the bar and the resurgence of the cultures of those deported as slaves. Limbo has been a painful experience for the dancer and the people but Brathwaite is proud of his ancestry and its resilience.

**16**

# Boost your grade: from D to C

## Poems from different cultures: cluster 2

p74 ⇨

This is the response to the essay question that you assessed on page 74 of the Student's Book. It was awarded a grade D. The annotations on the right show why the extract was awarded a D, and how you could turn it into a grade C. Words in bold are quoted from the examiner's assessment criteria.

---

**D grade: awareness of feeling(s), attitude(s) and ideas.**

To turn this into a grade C, you need to show which words/phrases in the poem help us to understand what the poet feels. For example:

*Although the poet wonders why her heart has been "unchained" by the hurricane, she also recognises that any reminder of her culture is reassuring because it makes her less homesick.*

This would fulfil the C grade criterion **understanding of feelings, attitudes and ideas.**

---

**D grade: some extended supported comment.**

To turn this into a C grade, you need to make your use of detail from the text more effective. For example:

*The speaker of the poem sees those around him being "dragged" away but does not care, emphasised by the refrain "What business ... savouring mouth".*

This would fulfil the C grade criterion **effective supporting use of textual detail.**

---

**D grade: range of comment supported by textual details.**

To turn this into a grade C, you need to make more reference to the text. For example:

*The names of the people in the poem, as well as the reference to "yams", suggest that the culture the poet is discussing is West African. In addition, "so long they don't take the yam" is written in African dialect.*

This would fulfil the C grade criterion **effective supporting use of textual detail.**

---

I am going to discuss the way that Grace Nichols and Niyi Osundare present culture in their poems "Hurricane Hits England" and "Not My Business". I intend to look at what is important to the poets about the cultures and what they are trying to say about them, from the language they use to describe them.

Grace Nichols's poem "Hurricane Hits England" is about just that, but it is what the storm means to the poet that what really matters. As hurricanes in England aren't normal, the poet is surprised by it and it reminds her of the Caribbean where they are more common. In a strange way, the hurricane makes her feel at home. She feels that the hurricane is speaking to her and freeing her from the feeling that she does not really belong in England but wonders why her heart has been "unchained" by such an event. Niyi Osundare seems to be talking about the what can happen if there's a culture where people only take care of themselves.

In the first three stanzas, there are stories of three people who are in some way attacked by the state without the reader knowing why. The speaker in the poem does not care because nothing has happened to him and "they" "haven't taken the food from his "savoring mouth". In the fourth stanza though, things change for the speaker. From the names of the people in the poem, you can tell that this is set in Africa and the speaker mentions "yams" which are a West African fruit.

GCSE English & Literature: Exam Preparation Support Pack © HarperCollins *Publishers* 2003

## Poems from different cultures: cluster 2

This is the response to the essay question that you assessed on page 80 of the Student's Book. It was awarded a grade B. The annotations on the right show why the extract was awarded a B, and how you could turn it into a grade A. Words in bold are quoted from the examiner's assessment criteria.

B grade: **understanding of a variety of writer's techniques.**

To turn this into an A grade, you need to explain more fully how the metaphor works. For example:

*At the start of the poem the speaker's fear of losing her ability to speak her native language, which forms an important part of her identity, is expressed in the metaphor "rot and die". However, by the end of the poem her confidence is restored by the bud which "pushes the other tongue aside" and enables the native language to "blossom".*

This would fulfil the A grade criterion **analysis of a variety of writer's techniques.**

B grade: **understanding of a variety of writer's techniques.**

To turn this into a grade A, you need to explain the effect of the image in more detail. For example:

*Pushing "the other tongue aside" recognises Gujerati as the mother tongue and as the more dominant language which grows in strength and beauty ("blossoms out of my mouth") the more it is used.*

This would fulfil the A grade criterion **analysis of a variety of writer's techniques.**

B grade: **appreciation of feelings, attitudes and ideas.**

To turn this into a grade A, you need to explain further what these attitudes and feelings say about the people who have them. For example:

*Leonard is angry that people think "thirza right way ti spell ana right way ti tok it". This exposes their snobbery and prejudice against a wide variety of accents and regional dialects, which are part of people's identity.*

This would fulfil the A grade criterion **exploration of and empathy with writer's ideas and attitudes.**

In "Search for My Tongue", Sujata Bhatt writes about the problem many bi-lingual people might face when they live away from the country where they grew up. The poet seem to be worried that she will forget her first language because she never speaks it. She sees language as more than just a simple means of communicating with people because it represents her original culture as well. You can tell that she is worried that she will forget the language and sees this as an entirely negative thing by the words that she uses. The idea that: "your mother tongue would rot, rot and die in your mouth" is an unpleasant image because having something rotting in your mouth would be physically sickening.

The extended metaphor in the last eight lines of the poem is in direct contrast to the ideas of sickness and decay. Bhatt likens Gujerati to a plant growing stronger until "it pushes the other tongue aside" and "blossoms out of my mouth". The poet clearly finds the experience of dreaming in Gujerati a reassuring one as it shows her that she has not lost touch with where she comes from.

Tom Leonard also writes about language but in a different way. Like Bhatt, he sees the way people speak as a way of telling which culture people come from but he does not like the way that people assume things about the class and intelligence of the speaker from the accent they use. He seems angry that the people who speak with a strong accent would not be newsreaders because people would not take them seriously, as though things that are important and reliable news can only be given in a "BBC accent". He is angry that people think "thirza right way ti spell ana right way ti tok it".

18

# Seamus Heaney

## The Perch – Seamus Heaney

The stillness of fish in a fast-moving stream is closely observed.

### Setting and context

- The poem is informed by the poet's personal experience, but does not have an autobiographical frame.
- The Bann river runs from the Mourne mountains to Loch Neagh in Northern Ireland. It is fast flowing and is used to produce hydro-electricity.

### Form and techniques

- The poem consists of 5 couplets using partial rhymes.
- There is a pun on the word 'perch', suggesting the name of the fish and their stillness in the river.
- 'Water-perch', 'water-roof' and 'air/That is water' suggest that Heaney sees the perch as birds in their equivalent of fast-flowing air.
- Sounds repeated with variations, such as 'runty and ready', 'I saw and I see' and 'finland ... fenland', give a smooth-flowing rhythm suggesting the fish's movement.
- 'Slubs' suggests slippery and smooth like the fish's movements, but also thick and uncompromising like a slab. The fish move and do not move.
- 'Adoze' is clearly formed by analogy with asleep. Dozing is less passive than sleeping – the fish do not move but they are alert.
- The phrase 'holding the pass' implies a brave military operation against the odds, such as the Spartans holding the pass at Thermopylae. It is clear that Heaney admires the perch for their persistence.
- 'Guzzling the current' suggests that the fish are larger than they really are, as if they were overcoming the river itself rather than simply existing in it.
- The musical associations of 'slur' suggest that the fish move gracefully.
- The pun on finland/Finland suggests that the river is not simply a narrow place but an entire underwater nation.
- The contrast between the fish on hold and everything else in the world being on the move shows how much Heaney admires the stillness of the fish. The constant movement is expressed in the smooth-flowing rhythm of the final line.

### Theme and interpretation

- Many of Heaney's poems admire permanence in an ever-changing world. The perch present a striking example of dynamic stillness.

### Good matches

- Clare's Sonnet, The Eagle, The Field-Mouse (animals)
- Inversnaid, The Eagle, October (natural imagery)

## Storm on the Island – Seamus Heaney

Islanders face up to a storm.

### Setting and context

- The bleak island that is the setting for this poem is presumably off the Irish coast.
- Unusually for Heaney, this poem does not appear to be autobiographical.

### Form and techniques

- Free verse in a single stanza. Regular rhythm, many run-on lines.
- The tone begins confidently but moves from boasting about preparedness to an admission of fears.
- There is also an attempt to take a positive view of difficult aspects of life on the island, e.g. 'The wizened earth has never troubled us/With hay'. The ground is clearly infertile, but the speaker makes it sound as if the lack of hay was a favour done to free the islanders from work
- Interesting shifts in view-point: 'I' is confessional, 'we' is usually confident of enduring, while 'you' invites the reader to share in the speaker's fears.
- The sea is described as 'exploding comfortably' – the 1st of the military images in the poem. Although it implies violence, because it is distant and familiar it is not threatening.
- The violence of the sea in the storm is emphasised by the difference between its normal power and strength and the idea of it spitting 'like a tame cat turned savage'. The violence seems worse because it comes from a familiar source.
- The final section returns to military imagery. The wind is like a fighter plane that 'dives and strafes', and space attacks like artillery in salvoes and a bombardment. In the face of these attacks the islanders can do nothing but sit tight until they are over.
- The oxymoron of a 'huge nothing' emphasises the paradox that the islanders are threatened by something that is invisible and in itself harmless.
- Alliteration of 's' echoes the sound of the wind at the end.

### Theme and interpretation

- This description of life in rural Ireland shows the harshness of a country existence and emphasises the impact of the elements on such people's lives.

### Good matches

- Patrolling Barnegat, Inversnaid, October (weather, effects on people)
- Patrolling Barnegat, The Eagle, October (sound, imagery)

## Death of a Naturalist – Seamus Heaney

A boy's attitude to frogs changes suddenly.

### Setting and context

- This 'autobiographical' poem relates a turning point in the speaker's childhood, identifying a precise moment when childhood innocence is lost.

### Form and techniques

- Unrhymed free verse in 2 irregular stanzas. The 1st stanza records the speaker's innocent vision of frogs, the 2nd a more sinister, adult view.
- Sound effects help to create the oppressive atmosphere at the beginning of the poem. Alliteration in 'flax-dam festered' emphasises decay. In 'green and heavy headed', 'sweltered in the punishing sun' and 'bluebottles/Wove a strong gauze of sound around the smell' attention is drawn to the sleepiness of the scene. The 'b' and 'g' sounds repeated in 'bubbles gargled delicately' give an impression of the quiet but suggest harsher undertones.
- The frogspawn is described with a great deal of enthusiasm. Phrases like 'warm, thick slobber' convey the child's enjoyment of gooey things.
- The run-ons in lines 13 to 15 show the speaker's enthusiasm overflowing the line.
- Children often assume that other people know what they do and would not think to explain that 'Miss Walls' (line 15) was the name of the class teacher.
- 'Daddy frog' and 'mammy frog' also reflect a child's point of view.
- The flax dam and its smell are passive and unmoving. The smell of cow dung suggests that other animals are intruding on the scene.
- The threat of the frogs is conveyed through military images such as 'invaded', 'cocked' (like a loaded gun) and 'mud grenades'.
- Harsh onomatopoeic sounds like 'slap and plop' are in sharp contrast to the earlier 'warm thick slobber' and reflect the harsher reality the speaker is facing.
- Disgust and unease is expressed through words like 'gross-bellied' and 'farting'.
- 'The great slime kings' are the same animals as the earlier frogs, but 'kings' implies that they are now in control and 'slime' marks them as being disgusting rather than fascinating.

### Theme and interpretation

- As the title suggests, this poem marks the end of a period in the speaker's life. This is the end of simple enjoyment of nature and the beginning of adult feelings of sexuality, responsibility and guilt.

### Good matches

- October, Ulysses, The Village Schoolmaster (change and decay)
- Clare's Sonnet, Patrolling Barnegat, October (natural imagery)

## Blackberry-Picking – Seamus Heaney

Picking blackberries is fun, but the berries will not last.

### Setting and context

- This 'autobiographical' poem reflects the joys and pains of childhood.
- Like many of Heaney's poems at this period, it reflects his dismay at the idea of change and decay.

### Form and techniques

- The poem consists of a series of couplets, using mostly half-rhymes, divided into 2 irregular stanzas. The 1st stanza describes the blackberry-picking, the 2nd describes how they rot.
- Blood imagery is established in line 3 and then extended as the poem continues: 'summer's blood' and 'lust for picking' suggest a vampire's attitude to the blackberries. The blackberry juice staining the pickers' hands suggests a link with the serial wife murderer Bluebeard.
- The list of receptacles used to collect the berries suggests by its rapid monosyllables the urgency of the desire to pick them.
- The list of places the pickers visit suggests their enthusiasm.
- The 'plate of eyes' image suggests both the bloodthirsty theme and the idea of a plate of delicacies.
- The alliteration of the 'f' and 's' sounds in stanza 2 emphasises the disgust felt by the speaker.
- The poem uses a full rhyme in lines 3 and 4 to emphasise the strength of the impression created by the first ripe berries.
- The same rhyme is used at the end to emphasise the speaker's disappointment.
- The phrase 'It wasn't fair' suggests a child's protest at the injustices of life.
- The last line of the poem represents a more adult tone of voice and point of view.

### Theme and interpretation

- The poem is concerned primarily with expressing one of the joys of childhood.
- However, the joy and enthusiasm of the 1st stanza is balanced by the disappointment and frustration of the 2nd.
- The 2nd stanza recognises the impossibility of stopping change and decay.

### Good matches

- October, Ulysses, The Village Schoolmaster (change and decay)
- Clare's Sonnet, Patrolling Barnegat, October (natural imagery)

20

## Digging – Seamus Heaney

A reflection on skills and talents in different generations.

### ▊ Setting and context

• This autobiographical poem recalls the achievements of Heaney's father and grandfather.

• Heaney cannot match his ancestors as diggers but he can write about them.

### ▊ Form and techniques

• Free verse, in irregular stanzas. Line length is used for emphasis at the end.

• Examples of onomatopoeia being used to create the poem's soundscape include: 'rasping sound', 'nicking and slicing neatly' and 'squelch and slap'. Sounds are often more evocative of a time and place than sights.

• Throughout the poem Heaney uses very precise language. This is in tribute to the precision of his father and grandfather. 'Nicking' is clearly a different activity from 'slicing' and the 'clean rasping sound' of digging in a garden is very different to the 'squelch and slap' of digging in a peat bog.

• The same precision is evident in memories of bottles 'corked sloppily with paper' and descriptions of potatoes and potato mould.

• Heaney's father and grandfather were experts with spades. Heaney hopes to be an expert with his pen.

• The poem begins and ends with descriptions of the pen with which it was written. Heaney has used it to 'dig' into his own past.

### ▊ Theme and interpretation

• In deciding to become a writer Heaney has to follow a different trade from his father and grandfather. In this poem he makes it clear that he has not rejected his past; he has merely adopted a different tool from that of his predecessors.

• Heaney's admiration for his father and grandfather is obvious. He hopes that their skill will be an inspiration to him, and the language of the poem is a testament to their skill and precision.

### ▊ Good matches

• Catrin, On My First Sonne, The Song of the Old Mother (parents and children)

• Sonnet 130, October (nature of writing)

## Mid-Term Break – Seamus Heaney

A boy returns from boarding school in the middle of term when his brother dies.

### ▊ Setting and context

• This poem records Heaney's response to the death of his brother Christopher in a car accident.

• Heaney was away at school when the accident happened.

### ▊ Form and techniques

• The traditional association of bells sounding with funerals helps to establish the sombre mood of the poem in the 1st stanza.

• This mood is also enhanced by the harsh alliteration of 'c' in 'counting', 'classes' and 'close' and the use of internal rhyme to slow down the pace of the line.

• Alliteration and assonance of harsh 'a' sounds in the 5th stanza help to convey the grimness of the arrival of the ambulance.

• The shock of seeing his brother is communicated by the monosyllables in line 20 which slow down the pace of the poem and make each word emphatic. This is further enhanced by the alliteration of 'f' and the assonance of 'o' in 'box and 'cot'.

• Language breaks down in the poem. Heaney's father cries and his mother 'coughed out angry tearless sighs', the baby 'coos' because it does not understand. Big Jim Evans's unfortunate pun on 'hard blow'reminds people of the accident rather than soothes. The neighbours resort to clichés. All of this suggests that language is powerless in the face of tragedy.

• The mood in the brother's room contrasts with the rest of the poem. The white flowers and gentle candle light are soothing and there is a traditional association of poppies with sleep.

• The lack of verbs (action words) in the last sentence underlines the lack of life in the little boy's body.

### ▊ Theme and interpretation

• This poem explores the impact of the sudden death of a child on the family.

• Words, quite literally, fail almost everyone, but Heaney finds a sense of peace when he sees his brother again.

### ▊ Good matches

• Mali, On My First Sonne, The Affliction of Margaret (family ties)

• October, On My First Sonne, Tichborne's Elegy (death)

• Baby-sitting, Little Boy Lost/Found, Song of the Old Mother (simple diction)

## At a Potato Digging – Seamus Heaney

Digging up potatoes and the significance of the activity.

### ● Setting and context

- The poem describes people digging potatoes in the present day, with a flashback to the past.
- Their behaviour and attitudes are still influenced by the 1845 potato blight which caused crops to fail. Over a million people died and millions more fled the country.

### ● Form and techniques

- The poem is divided into 4 parts. Parts 1 and 4 refer to the present day and use quatrains with an abab rhyme scheme. Part 2 describes a healthy potato harvest and has 2 unequal stanzas using some full and some half rhymes. Part 3 describes Ireland in 1845 in 5 quatrains with an aabb rhyme scheme. The couplets in this section make it the most emphatic.
- Heaney connects harvesting the land with harvesting the sea with images such as 'creels' and 'fish a new load from the crumbled surf'.
- The black-clad workers are compared to crows gathering round a food supply.
- Religious terms such as 'processional', 'homage', 'altar' and 'libations' show that the workers regard their task as deeply serious and significant.
- In part 2 words like 'hearts', 'cream' and 'a clean birth' all emphasise the goodness and importance of the crop.

- The transition from part 2 to part 3 is achieved by repeating a line but, shockingly, the blind-eyed skulls belong to people rather than potatoes.
- In part 3 famine is compared to a scavenging bird snipping at stomachs.
- Words such as 'rotted', 'stinking', 'pus' and 'sore' present a picture of the blight as both a potato disease and an illness that affected the country itself.
- 'Breaking timeless fasts' refers to the act of eating for the first time on the day described and to the fact that the harvest will prevent future fasting.
- Both 'mother' (part 1) and 'bitch' (part 3) acknowledge the earth as the source of life. The second term implies that the earth doesn't care about its offspring.
- The workers' offering of 'libations' to the earth shows that they treat the earth as a sort of pagan goddess.

### ● Theme and interpretation

- The poem connects past suffering with present day behaviour and belief.
- The people of Northern Ireland have an almost pagan relationship with the soil that supports them. They depend upon it and treat it with both fear and respect.

### ● Good matches

- Inversnaid, Patrolling Barnegat, The Field-Mouse (nature)
- The Man He Killed, The Laboratory, Inversnaid, Cold Knap Lake (use of rhyme)

---

## Follower – Seamus Heaney

Old age reverses the roles of father and son.

### ● Setting and context

- Like 'Digging', this poem explores Heaney's relationship with his father, using the farm as a backdrop and as a source of imagery.
- Heaney clearly admired his father and is saddened by the changes brought about by old age.

### ● Form and techniques

- Regular 4-line stanzas with an abab rhyme scheme. Some full and some half-rhymes.
- Several images describe the father in terms of a ship navigating the fields, e.g. 'shoulders globed like a full sail', 'hob-nailed wake' and 'dipping and rising to his plod'. These give an impression of the size and importance of his father to the young Heaney and also imply grace, strength and dependability.
- The father's control over powerful horses through his 'clicking tongue' or a 'single pluck' emphasises his skill and absolute mastery of his craft.
- Run-on lines are used for emphasis. A word or phrase is left isolated at the end of a line, forcing a slight pause while the eye travels back for the next word, e.g. 'His eye' and 'But today'.
- In contrast the run on between stanzas 2 and 3 demonstrates the smoothness and power of the father's control over the horses.

- The isolated words 'An expert' make Heaney's assessment of his father stand out. The lack of verb implies that there is nothing more that needs to be said.
- Heaney's use of partial rhymes gives the poem a lighter tone than it might have had with full rhymes.
- Heaney's use of technical terms to do with horse ploughs demonstrates the same kind of precision with words that his father showed in his ploughing.
- The 3 verbs 'tripping, falling, yapping' give a sense of the young Heaney's energy, but also of his relative clumsiness. They suggest a young puppy.
- The final phrase of the poem could be taken literally or relate to the poet's memory. In either case the change has been brought about by the passage of time.

### ● Theme and interpretation

- Time and decay appear once again as the great villains in Heaney's poetry.
- The power and strength of Heaney's father have been taken away by time and the roles of parent and child have been reversed.

### ● Good matches

- Mali, On My First Sonne, The Affliction of Margaret (family ties)
- The Man He Killed, The Laboratory, Inversnaid (use of rhyme)

## Catrin – Gillian Clarke

A mother recalls the birth of her child and later struggles.

### Setting and context

- This poem is autobiographical.
- The 1st section deals with the birth of Catrin; in the 2nd part she is old enough to want some independence.

### Form and technique

- Free verse in a single stanza. There is a time shift but there is no break in the poem, indicating that there is no break in the experience of motherhood.
- The 1st part is characterised by images of heat, the 2nd uses colder images.
- The descriptions in the 1st part demonstrate the fact that people tend to remember small details at moments of intense emotion.
- The birth itself seems to isolate the speaker from the people in the street who are on the other side of the window. The heat of the room contrasts with the colder, calmer outside so that condensation forms on the glass.
- The fact that the daughter wants to spend more time skating shows that she wants to move away from the heat of their relationship into the colder outer world.

- In the labour ward the mother brings sound and colour to the 'environmental blank'. This is a metaphor for the process of giving birth itself and it anticipates the early life of the baby.
- The umbilical cord is a physical 'red rope of love' which becomes a metaphorical 'old rope ... trailing love and conflict' later in the poem. This reflects the changing nature of the bond between mothers and children – more physical at first, more emotional later.

### Theme and interpretation

- The poem suggests that mothers and children are connected in a way that isolates them from the world. However, as the child grows older s/he needs to go out into the wider world.
- The bond between mother and child is a sort of umbilical cord that must be cut eventually if the child is to prosper.

### Good matches

- Follower, The Song of the Old Mother, On My First Sonne (parents and children)
- Digging, Ulysses, The Eagle (use of imagery)

---

## Baby-sitting – Gillian Clarke

A baby-sitter worries about the baby.

### Setting and context

- This poem appears to be autobiographical.
- It deals with the common anxiety felt by baby-sitters that they will not be able to comfort the baby if it wakes. Unusually it looks at the world from the baby's viewpoint.

### Form and technique

- Unrhymed free verse in 2 stanzas – the 1st few lines deal with the sitter's thoughts and feelings, the rest deals with the baby's feelings and reactions.
- The poem imagines that the baby's feelings will be violent and uses words such as 'hate', 'shout' and 'rage' to describe them in the 1st stanza.
- In the 2nd stanza she uses 2 comparisons to describe the baby's feeling of abandonment: a deserted lover, and a grieving woman at her husband's (?) deathbed.
- These extreme feelings contrast strongly with the quiet, 'snuffly roseate, bubbling' sleeping baby.
- The baby-sitter's feelings are more moderate: she is 'afraid' of the baby but for her it is just the 'wrong' baby who will 'fail to enchant' her.
- The difference between the 2 sets of feelings is possibly explained by experience. The baby does not know that her mother will return and so reacts as if she has been abandoned.

- The 2nd stanza uses a number of sound effects for emphasis: 'absolute/Abandonment' is an alliterative run on; the longing of the deserted 'lover cold in lonely/Sheets' is underlined by alliteration of 'l' and the slight pause before 'sheets'; the sentence on the woman runs over 3 lines but does not make sense until the final word; this sense of suspense is added to by the alliteration of 'b' towards the end; the baby's distress is indicated by the hissing alliteration of 's' in lines 17–18.
- The repeated 'It will not come' suggests that the connection between a mother and a baby is not something that can be forced.

### Theme and interpretation

- This poem looks beyond conventions – baby-sitters are supposed to like the children they mind and babies are meant to be innocent, lovable, gentle creatures.
- The baby-sitter is at best ambivalent about the child, and the baby feels emotions that are as devastating and serious as anything an adult might feel.

### Good matches

- The Song of the Old Mother, Little Boy Lost/Found, Mid-Term Break (adults and children)
- Digging, Ulysses, The Eagle (use of imagery)

## Mali – Gillian Clarke

A grandmother celebrates her granddaughter.

### Setting and context

- This poem is autobiographical.
- It deals with the circumstances surrounding the birth of the poet's granddaughter.

### Form and techniques

- The monthly cycle of the moon which causes the 'tug of the tide' (line 2) is a reference to the pull of childbirth across the generations. (Menstruation is another monthly cycle.)
- The speaker is surprised that this 'tug' is still there. The birth of her granddaughter has a stronger effect on her than she imagined.
- A harvest moon (line 16) is the full moon nearest to the autumnal equinox. The granddaughter appears at the transition from the 'summer' to the 'autumn' of the speaker's life.
- The sea couldn't draw the speaker from her granddaughter (line 21) because their bond was so strong. The reference is to resisting the pull of the sea.
- The poet's love is assumed to be weakened by age, but in fact the latter end of the year is a time of fruit and abundance.
- The grandmother blossoms like an old tree (line 23). Something beautiful has come from her late in life.
- The blood at the end of the poem suggests the blood ties that bind the 3 women. From the grandmother's point of view it is also a reference to the end of menstruation.

### Theme and interpretation

- This poem investigates the bond between the poet and her grandchild. It is much more positive than either Catrin or Baby-sitting as it reflects a connection that is close but not too close.
- The poem is also about a late blossoming in the poet's life – a reminder of the physical and emotional bonds of childbirth.

### Good matches

- Mid-Term Break, On My First Sonne, The Affliction of Margaret (parent and child)
- Clare's Sonnet, Patrolling Barnegat, Death of a Naturalist (natural imagery)

## A Difficult Birth, Easter 1998 – Gillian Clarke

The birth of lambs at Easter prompts thoughts about politics and religion.

### Setting and context

- This poem is apparently autobiographical.
- It refers to the Good Friday agreement of 1998 which sought to bring peace to Northern Ireland, to the Easter uprising in Dublin in 1916 and to the first Easter.

### Form and techniques

- Unrhymed 6-line stanzas. Flexible rhythm. The final line is short for emphasis.
- The fact that the speaker is attending the birth of a lamb prompts a connection with Jesus, 'the Lamb of God'. The lamb is also a traditional Christian symbol of peace.
- The poem suggests that the struggle for independence in Ireland since 1916 has been marked by pain. The Good Friday agreement is as difficult and exhausting a 'birth' as the birth of the lamb.
- The 2nd lamb 'slips through' easily. This suggests that the future of Ireland will be easier if the Good Friday agreement succeeds.
- The birth is exclusively a female concern.
- The metonym 'whitecoats' suggests the scientific approach but it also implies sterility and the refusal to get involved in the messy business of birth.
- The doctors' instruments suggest distance and pain ('needles' and 'forceps') which contrasts with the empathic 'hands on' approach of the speaker.
- The political message of the poem seems to be that politics might achieve its aim more often if women are involved.
- The imagery concerning the lamb uses ideas of wetness and dryness. The waters are a 'lost salty ocean', the lamb comes in a 'syrupy flood' and the mother 'drinks' the lamb. These positive, watery images are in opposition to the sheep's 'burning tongue' which indicates its distress before the lamb arrives.
- As well as the re-birth of Christ at Easter, the lamb's birth reminds the reader of his birth in a stable at Christmas.
- The phrase 'a cradling that might have been a death' reminds the reader that all births are potentially hazardous.

### Theme and interpretation

- The idea of birth is a very positive one but the poem reminds the reader that birth is also a time of great danger.
- The poem connects the birth of the lambs with political events in an optimistic fashion – perhaps the difficult birth of the Good Friday agreement could also be a success.

### Good matches

- Inversnaid, Patrolling Barnegat, Storm on the Island (nature)
- At a Potato Digging, Clare's Sonnet, Tichborne's Elegy (use of natural imagery)

## October – Gillian Clarke

The death of a friend inspires the speaker to work harder.

### Setting and context

- This poem is autobiographical.
- It concerns the death of the poet's friend, Frances Horovitz.

### Form and technique

- The poem is in 3 irregular unrhymed stanzas. Line 12 is broken over 2 stanzas: it marks the poem's shift from past to present.
- The month of October, towards the end of the year, is associated with the end of a life. Other images in the 1st stanza, such as the broken branch, the changing of the leaves and the fading of the colours in the statue, prefigure ideas of old age and death.
- The age of the friend is suggested by the description 'lighter than hare-bones', as if she had grown thin and insubstantial before she died.
- The people are transformed into statues ('faces stony') by their grief, while the rain expresses it through 'weeping'.
- Other striking images: 'poplars tremble gradually to gold' suggests an image of growing old that is both weak and dignified; 'the grave deep as a well' – wells are deep but they are also sources of refreshment: the friend's death encourages the poet to write; 'faster than wind's white steps over grass' compares the act of writing with the speedy change brought about by the wind on grass; 'year after year passing my death-day' reminds the reader that we pass the date of our death on the calendar every year – it is just a question of in which year we will die.
- The final part of the poem lists some of the things that need to be captured – they are similar to items earlier in the poem and confirm that the poem is inspired by the poet's resolution to gain some ground on death before she dies.

### Theme and interpretation

- This poem looks at death in nature and for human beings.
- The death represented by winter is always a re-birth in spring, but death for humans is permanent.
- The only thing we can do is to leave something permanent behind like poetry.

### Good matches

- Mid-Term Break, The Man He Killed, On My First Sonne, Tichborne's Elegy (dealing with death)
- Storm on the Island, Clare's Sonnet, Patrolling Barnegat (natural imagery)

## The Field-Mouse – Gillian Clarke

The death of a field-mouse prompts thoughts on peace and war.

### Setting and context

- This poem is autobiographical.
- In the background there are references to the war in the former Yugoslavia (1990s).

### Form and technique

- The poem is in 3 regular 9-line stanzas.
- It connects everyday events with those happening in the wider world by contrasting the peace on the farm with the terrible events on the radio.
- The peaceful description is deceptive, though. The grass is like a 'snare drum' used by marching soldiers, and the air is 'humming' with jets instead of bees.
- Pain makes itself felt through the field-mouse. The children think the adults can deal with its suffering but they are powerless, just as we are powerless in the face of suffering in war.
- The field is personified as if it were some injured 'bleeding animal' and the animals coming from it are compared to refugees. The cutting of the grass in the field is as devastating for its inhabitants as a war is for humans.
- The connection between the injured mouse and the speaker's children is made by the simile 'bones brittle as mouse-ribs'. This suggests the speaker's anxiety about what would happen to them if war suddenly erupted as it did in the former Yugoslavia.
- The idea of civil war is suggested by the neighbour 'wounding my land with stones'.

### Theme and interpretation

- The poem is about the fragility of life and the fragility of peace.
- The peaceful scene does not guarantee safety, as the inhabitants of Yugoslavia discovered, and if war does break out there is little that adults can do to protect their children.
- The fragile field-mouse represents both peace and the children themselves.

### Good matches

- Storm on the Island, The Man He Killed, Patrolling Barnegat (war and violence)
- Storm on the Island, Clare's Sonnet, Patrolling Barnegat (natural imagery)

# Gillian Clarke

## On the Train – Gillian Clarke

An anxious train user phones home.

### Setting and context

- This poem is autobiographical.
- It was written after the Paddington train crash of October 1999.

### Form and technique

- 4 unrhymed, 6-line stanzas, with various train-like rhythms.
- The regular rhythm, repetition and alliteration in the 1st stanza are intended to remind the reader of the sound and rhythm of a train.
- The 'blazing bone-ship' (line 12) could be a direct reference to a train heading towards an accident involving fire. The idea of passengers being reduced to bones emphasises the heat of the blaze stripping away flesh. The 'blazing bone-ship' may also refer to a Viking funeral. In this case the passengers are only heading towards death in the same way that everyone is.
- The language used by the Vodaphone answering service is neutral and devoid of anything other than its surface meaning. However, its very ordinariness makes it sound chilling in the context of the disaster the speaker imagines.
- Since there are no wolves left in England, the idea of them howling down phones implies a complete breakdown of civilisation.
- The speaker's anxiety is conveyed by the choppy rhythm of the separate sentences at the beginning of the 4th stanza.
- The final line of the poem gives an annoying cliché new force and real meaning in the context of the anxiety that has just been expressed.

### Theme and interpretation

- The poem deals with the anxiety felt by someone separated from his or her loved one.
- Its language contrasts contemporary brand names such as 'Vodaphone' and 'Walkman' and modern clichés with more primitive images of disaster.
- The poem reminds us that despite technological advances we are never very far away from disaster.

### Good matches

- The Affliction of Margaret, Little Boy Lost/Found, Follower (worry about loved one)
- Digging, Tichborne's Elegy, On My First Sonne (1st-person point of view)

---

## Cold Knap Lake – Gillian Clarke

A disturbing childhood memory – or is it?

### Setting and context

- This poem is autobiographical.
- It is set at Cold Knap Lake, a local beauty spot in Barry, Glamorgan, south Wales.

### Form and technique

- The poem is in 5 irregular stanzas. Half-rhyme is used throughout, except for full rhyme in the final couplet – an emphatic ending.
- A linear narrative structure – suspense is created by holding back information about whether the 'drowned' girl is alive or not.
- The expression 'gave ... her breath' makes the mother appear active; there is a hint of jealousy from the speaker because the breath is given to a stranger's child.
- Alliteration of 'd' at the end of the 2nd stanza is emphatic and hints at doom; this creates tension before it is revealed that the child is alive.
- The line 'Was I there?' stands out because it is shorter than all the others. It is also the central question of the poem. Is this a real memory or is it something that the speaker has been told?
- The final stanza suggests that memory is like the surface of the lake; all kinds of things enter it and stir it up but all we can see is the surface.
- The emphatic final couplet sounds like a proverb or a nursery rhyme: perhaps a general piece of wisdom is being provided, though it is as mysterious as the lake.

### Theme and interpretation

- The theme of this poem is memory.
- The 1st part of the incident is full of circumstantial detail and seems to have been witnessed by the speaker. The 2nd part is less detailed and the speaker is unsure if she was there.
- The surface of the lake is a metaphor for the uncertainty of memory. Some details are clear but others are clouded by the passage of time.

### Good matches

- Ulysses, My Last Duchess, Digging (memories)
- Mid-Term Break, Tichborne's Elegy, The Affliction of Margaret (sorrowful tone)

## Elvis's Twin Sister – Carol Ann Duffy

A less famous Presley contemplates fame and contentment.

### Setting and context

- Elvis Aaron Presley is perhaps the most famous rock and roll singer of all time.
- Since his death in 1977 there have been numerous claims that he is alive and well.

### Form and techniques

- Regular 5-line stanzas with some very short lines. 1st-person perspective.
- The 2 quotations at the beginning provide an excuse for the poem and introduce its 2 themes: loneliness and the life of a 'sister'.
- The poem captures the way Elvis spoke through southern American slang such as 'y'all' and 'Lawdy'. This contrasts with the sister's use of Latin and her references to Gregorian chant. The idea that the Reverend Mother digs the way the speaker moves her hips is amusing.
- Allusions to songs such as 'Blue Suede Shoes', 'Heartbreak Hotel' and 'Are You Lonesome Tonight?' remind readers of Elvis's songs. The second 2 songs refer to loneliness and heartbreak – something that does not trouble the quiet sister.

- The allusion to Graceland, Elvis's home, allows the speaker to introduce a religious interpretation of the word 'grace'. The sister seems to have found it whereas Elvis did not.
- Run-ons are used for humorous effect. Conclusions to stanzas such as 'of rock 'n' roll' and 'blue suede shoes' are unexpected in the context and therefore amusing.
- The poem varies in tone between amusing and unhappy – this is shown in Elvis's lyrics.

### Theme and interpretation

- The poem contrasts fame and obscurity. Elvis's twin sister has chosen obscurity but found grace and contentment.
- Elvis seems to have wanted grace but did not achieve it.

### Good matches

- The Laboratory, Ulysses, My Last Duchess, Kid (1st-person persona)

---

## Havisham – Carol Ann Duffy

A jilted woman curses the man who abandoned her.

### Setting and context

- Miss Havisham is a character from Dickens's novel *Great Expectations*.
- She has gone mad as the result of having been jilted on her wedding day. Since that day, time has not moved on for her.

### Form and techniques

- Regular 4-line stanzas. 1st-person perspective.
- The title, 'Havisham', strips her of her title 'Miss', just as the lover did, but does not replace it with 'Mrs' as should have happened.
- Oxymorons such as 'beloved sweetheart bastard,' and 'love's hate' reveal the opposing emotions that Miss Havisham feels.
- 'Spinster' is emphasised by being placed on its own. The absence of a verb shows the lack of activity in her life as a spinster.
- Miss Havisham is like a bird 'cawing' at the wall. Later she loses the power of speech, uttering 'sounds not words'. In both cases she is less than human.
- The words 'Nooooo' and 'b-b-b-breaks' both show how damaged and distorted Miss Havisham's language has become since she was deserted. The 1st example suggests endless regret and the 2nd a complete loss of fluency.

- As well as the deterioration in sound and language, the sense of sight is evoked in the description of her eyes as 'dark green pebbles' and the sense of smell in 'I stink'. Touch is most evident in her dream encounter.
- Miss Havisham confuses sight and sound: 'puce curses' is 'synaesthesia' – both a poetic device and a sign of mental disturbance.
- When she looks in the mirror Miss Havisham says 'her, myself, who did this to me?' This shows confusion about her own identity as well as confronting the reader with the question of who has caused her present state, herself or the lover.
- The application of 'Bang' to 'red balloon bursting' and stabbing the wedding cake neatly links the breaking of her heart, the moment of its breaking and her mental state.

### Theme and interpretation

- This poem suggests that Miss Havisham's continued hatred of the man who jilted her is based on continued love.
- Miss Havisham seems to be the victim of much of her hatred.

### Good matches

- The Laboratory, Ulysses, My Last Duchess, Hitcher (1st-person persona)
- Those bastards ..., Patrolling Barnegat, The Laboratory (powerful imagery)

GCSE English & Literature: Exam Preparation Support Pack © HarperCollins *Publishers* 2003

## Anne Hathaway – Carol Ann Duffy

Shakespeare's widow looks back on their life together.

### Setting and context

- Anne Hathaway was the wife of William Shakespeare.
- In the Elizabethan period the best bed would have been reserved for guests, and so the second best bed would have been the one that a married couple shared.
- Apart from plays, Shakespeare wrote 153 sonnets. Shakespearean sonnets are characterised by the use of a rhyming couplet at the end.
- Dead bodies are normally placed in caskets of coffins. Anne Hathaway's head is the physical location of her husband's spirit, just as the bed was the place where Shakespeare 'created' her. Even in death their mutual love survives.
- The poem is written as a Shakespearean sonnet, although it does not use a full Shakespearean rhyme scheme.
- The only full rhyme is the emphatic final couplet.

### Form and techniques

- The poem is a 14-line sonnet with a rhyming couplet at the end.
- It consists of a series of comparisons. The bed is compared to a world which resembles those created by Shakespeare in his plays.
- Shakespeare's words are compared to bright, fast-moving shooting stars.
- Anne Hathaway's body is a rhyme that echoes those of her husband.
- Shakespeare's touch is compared to an active verb.
- The bed with Anne Hathaway in it is like a page created by her husband. Together they create their own sensual dramas.
- In contrast, the guests staying in the other bed produce only prose.

### Theme and interpretation

- The poem undermines the myth that Anne Hathaway's marriage to Shakespeare was cool and distant.
- The poem's playful use of imagery, affectionate tone and sincere emotion reflect Anne Hathaway's love and loss.

### Good matches

- Homecoming, Sonnet 130, My Last Duchess (male–female relationships)
- Clare's Sonnet, Sonnet 130, Those bastards ... (sonnet form)

## Salome – Carol Ann Duffy

The famous dancer wakes up to find a head in her bed.

### Setting and context

- Salome, the daughter of Herodias, danced for King Herod and gained the head of John the Baptist as payment.
- In this version of the story Salome wakes with the head beside her. Usually it is brought into the palace on a platter.
- In the New Testament Peter, Simon, Andrew and John (lines 14–15) were disciples of Jesus. This Salome is not interested in either ancient or modern religious figures, only men.

### Theme and interpretation

- This modern version of Salome looks at the morning after the event that made her famous.
- She herself has no memory of the occasion and is as shocked as the reader to find John the Baptist's head in her bed.
- Salome has therefore used her talents as a dancer and her role as a woman to get what her mother wants.
- This Salome is an embodiment of thoughtless sexuality and its unpleasant consequences.

### Form and techniques

- Irregular stanzas and irregular verse (appropriate for someone with a hangover?). Line and stanza length used for emphasis. Only lines that end in '-ter' rhyme.
- The poem makes striking use of anachronism. Salome talks like a modern girl waking up after a night on the town. She enjoys a typically English breakfast of tea and toast and smokes tobacco over 1000 years before it appeared in Europe. All these things suggest that human behaviour changes little over time.
- The tone of the poem is not serious. Jokey colloquial language such as 'hungover and wrecked' and 'turf out the blighter' establish a rueful but light-hearted tone.
- The rhyme scheme teasingly reminds the reader of one of the best-known facts about John the Baptist: his head ended up on a platter.

### Good matches

- The Laboratory, My Last Duchess, Hitcher (killers – male and female)
- Ulysses, Kid, Those bastards ..., My Last Duchess (characters from history, myth or legend)

GCSE English & Literature: Exam Preparation Support Pack © HarperCollins *Publishers* 2003

# Carol Ann Duffy

## We Remember Your Childhood Well – Carol Ann Duffy

Parents disagree with their child about their shared past.

### Setting and context

- The poem is half of a conversation between a child and her parents.
- The parents are responding to the child's accusations about her past.

### Form and techniques

- Regular 3-line stanzas, and some near rhymes such as moors/door, fear/tears.
- The child's voice is absent. This implies that the child had no 'voice' when growing up.
- The child's views are only allowed into the poem so that they can be denied.
- The parents use a number of persuasive strategies: flat denial, slightly different interpretations of events, claims of great wisdom and insight and protestations that they were acting in the best interests of the child.
- The lines 'a Film Fun laughing itself to death in the coal fire' (lines 5–6) present an adult attempt to see the world from a child's point of view. The words 'anyone's guess' reinforce the fact that this is an imaginative reconstruction.
- The parents distinguish between impressions and facts. This is not a logical distinction – our impressions are the truth as far as we are concerned.
- The language of oppression reinforces the parents' bullying tone.
- The repeated 'Boom. Boom. Boom' (line 12) reminds the child of the difference in power between herself and her parents.
- Skidmarks (line 16) are evidence of something dangerous happening long ago. The evidence of damage done to the child remains.
- The rapid succession of short sentences at the end implies an attempt by the parents to close the discussion by not listening to any more of the child's responses.

### Theme and interpretation

- The child's attempt to share her memories is met with incomprehension and denial. The poem is really about power.
- Just as the parents had power in the past, they now claim power over how memories should be interpreted. They claim to be benign but they resort to bullying in the end. The poem acknowledges that people remember things differently, but the parents' insistence on their version of the 'truth' is disturbing.

### Good matches

- I've made out a will, Ulysses, Tichborne's Elegy (summing up life)
- My Last Duchess, The Laboratory, Kid (dramatic monologue)

---

## Before You Were Mine – Carol Ann Duffy

A daughter looks back at her mother's life.

### Setting and context

- The references to polka dots and Marilyn Monroe date the poem to the late 1950s.
- The speaker and her mother are Catholics living in Glasgow.
- Unusually for Carol Ann Duffy, this poem appears to be autobiographical.

### Form and techniques

- Regular, unrhymed, 5-line stanzas. Extensive use of run-on lines.
- The first 2 stanzas deal with the memories the mother has shared with her daughter.
- The second 2 stanzas deal with the daughter's life and memories of her mother.
- The mother's memories concern youth, freedom and glamour; the child's memories are to do with the relics of that glamour.
- The rhythm in the 2nd line of stanza 2 makes use of polysyllabic words like 'fizzy, movie tomorrows' to produce an air of excitement. In the last 2 lines of the final stanza 'and' is used to give a strong, dance-like rhythm.
- The placing of 'high-heeled red shoes' next to 'relics' presents a bathetic contrast between the mother's past and the daughter's present.
- The synaesthetic image 'I see you, clear as scent' treats sight as if it were smell. This is surprising and convincing, as memories are often more strongly evoked by smell rather than sight.
- The pauses at the end of the stanzas are moments of reflection or summing up before moving on. In the last stanza there is a smooth transition to the current situation where the mother belongs to the daughter.
- The frequent 'I' sounds in the last 2 lines of the poem have to be spoken carefully but emphatically. They add to the idea of enjoyment and lingering pleasure at this stage of the poem.

### Theme and interpretation

- The poem reflects on the difference between parents as they are and as they were.
- Although she lives in the strict and austere 1950s and early 1960s the mother's teenage years seem more glamorous than the daughter's.
- The child seems to want her mother both as she is and as she was.

### Good matches

- Mother, any distance …, The Song of the Old Mother, Little Boy Lost/Found, The Affliction of Margaret (mothers and children)
- Mother, any distance … On My First Sonne, Tichborne's Elegy, The Affliction of Margaret (1st-person statements)

## Stealing – Carol Ann Duffy

A thief discusses his more unusual thefts.

### Setting and context

- The setting for this poem is also deliberately vague. Is this a confession at a police station, a conversation with a therapist or a casual chat in a pub?
- Given the isolated life of the speaker, it is unlikely to be chat with a friend.

### Form and techniques

- The poem uses regular, unrhymed 5-line stanzas. Effective use is made of run-on lines.
- The poet establishes a conversational tone to the poem, varying its pace. In stanza 1 the speaker's enthusiasm runs from line to line, but in stanza 4 his frustration is shown by sentences that eventually break down into single words.
- An impression of ordinary speech is also created by the use of colloquial terms like 'mate', 'nick', 'gut', 'mucky', 'daft' and 'flogged'.
- The speaker seems to be a very cold person. This idea is explored in several different aspects of the poem. There is a 'winter moon' and 'ice' in the speaker's brain. The 'ghost', 'mirrors' and 'a bust of Shakespeare' all suggest human appearance but lack warmth.
- The fact that he thinks a snowman can be a 'mate' reinforces the connection between coldness and loneliness. The snowman, the guitar and the bust of Shakespeare all represent failed attempts at communication.
- Internal rhyme is used in 'slice of ice' and 'chill ... thrill'. The rhymes appear in the early optimistic part of the poem and are to do with coldness. A rhyme is a connection between two words and at this stage in the poem the speaker is trying to make a connection with the snowman.
- In contrast to the rhymes, later on in the poem words like 'Mirrors', 'Again' and 'Boredom' stand isolated in sentences of their own.
- The speaker tends to end each stanza with a short sentence which describes what is being done or makes a comment ('Life's tough', 'sick of the world'). The last line is addressed directly to the listener and suggests that this particular conversation has been yet another failed attempt at communication.

### Theme and interpretation

- The speaker doesn't seem able to connect with other people.
- Although he is a thief he cannot resist leaving clues about his presence. He also steals things that give a promise of contact.
- All his attempts at contact, even the poem itself, are judged by the speaker to be failures.

### Good matches

- Hitcher, My Last Duchess, Ulysses (isolated characters)
- Kid, My Last Duchess, Ulysses (dramatic monologues)

## Education for Leisure – Carol Ann Duffy

A disaffected young man contemplates killing.

### Setting and context

- The setting for this poem is deliberately anonymous; part of the boy's problem is that there is nothing particularly good or particularly bad about his life.
- 'Education for leisure' was an idea popular in the 1980s – that education should help people to cope with unemployment.

### Form and techniques

- Regular, unrhymed quatrains. Persona, use of the present tense and an implied listener are all features of dramatic monologues.
- The present tense narrative is immediate and vivid. It is especially shocking when the implied listener is the reader.
- The references to the past – being ignored, school days and going into town to sign on – give a more detailed picture of the speaker and provide some explanation of why he feels as he does.
- Verbless sentences like 'Anything', 'Shakespeare' and 'Something's world' lack an 'action' word just as the speaker's life lacks action.
- The words also appear as afterthoughts to the sentences that precede them. This gives an impression of the thought processes of someone who is often alone.
- Following 'today I am going to change the world' with 'Something's world' is an example of bathos – a big build-up followed by a trivial conclusion – and it shows the difference between the speaker's thoughts and reality.
- Other examples of bathos are 'I am a genius. I could be anything at all, with half the chance' (lines 9–10) and 'I ... tell the man he's talking to a superstar. He cuts me off' (lines 17–19).
- The allusions to Shakespeare and the Bible emphasise the gap between the speaker's education and his life. They are great books but all they do is give him grand ideas to explain his small actions – playing god is killing something, and killing a fly reminds him of a line from *King Lear*.

### Theme and interpretation

- This is a portrait of someone in a listless but dangerous state of mind.
- The speaker's education has not equipped him for a life of unemployment; he missed the point of the Bible and gained nothing from reading Shakespeare.

### Good matches

- Hitcher, My Last Duchess, The Laboratory (murderers)
- Kid, My Last Duchess, Ulysses (dramatic monologues)

## My father thought it bloody queer – Simon Armitage

A father's comments about jewellery come back to haunt the speaker.

### Setting and context
- This is from *A Book of Matches* and is therefore short and to the point.
- It seems to be autobiographical.

### Form and techniques
- Sonnet-like poem, with irregular line length and an irregular rhyme scheme.
- The section on the father has a strong rhythm and a clear, end-stopped rhyme scheme. This, and the use of the mild expletive 'bloody', suggest that the father was a forceful, no-nonsense, figure.
- The father uses a metaphor (ring in nose = easily lead) to express his criticism.
- His use of the word 'queer' shows either insensitivity to language trends or confidence in his own language use.
- The son is less forceful than the father. The later internal rhymes show less confidence.
- Pun on the word 'nerve' in stanza 2 draws attention to the son's uncertainty. If he didn't have nerves in his ear he would not feel pain.
- Progress from piercing to infection is described in a single sentence as if the process was inevitable.
- The simile used to describe the voice breaking ('like a tear') indicates something welling up from inside.
- There is strong emotion in the image of a tear evoked by the memory of a sound – perhaps the father is dead.
- The speaker claiming his father's words indicates that as he has grown older he has internalised some of his father's ideas and ways of expressing himself.

### Theme and interpretation
- The poem explores the way in which opinions change as we grow older.
- The youthful rebellion of the teenager seems ridiculous to the 29-year-old.
- The speaker finds himself agreeing with his father who was meant to shocked by the earring, but merely says it was following a fashion.
- The speaker admits also that he wasn't very good at following the fashion in the first place.

### Good matches
- On My First Sonne, Little Boy Lost/Little Boy Found, We Remember Your Childhood Well (parental attitudes)
- Sonnet 130, Clare's Sonnet, Anne Hathaway (sonnet uses and variations, rhyme, repetition)

## Mother, any distance – Simon Armitage

A young man is helped by his mother to measure up his new home.

### Setting and context
- Each poem in *A Book of Matches* is meant to be read in the time taken by a match to burn down.
- Several seem to be autobiographical.

### Form and techniques
- Stanzas 1 and 2 have 4 lines each; stanza 3 has 7 lines. There is some rhyme. Matchbook format resembles a sonnet in terms of compression.
- Lists used in all 3 sections to emphasise the unending nature of the task.
- Exaggeration of 'prairies' and 'acres' reinforces this idea (line 4).
- 'Anchor. Kite' (line 8) sums up the relationship between mother and son. He attempts to fly, she keeps him from flying away completely.
- However, a kite is only partially free to fly, and an anchor, though safe, is also a restriction. Both images are ambiguous.
- The single-word sentences are emphatic and demonstrate the separation of the people concerned in the relationship.
- 'Space-walk' (line 9) is another image that implies both freedom and being tethered.
- The tape measure at 'breaking point' implies that the connection between the mother and son is also in crisis – he is setting up his own home.
- The word 'pinch' (line 12) implies that the mother's hold on the son is felt as restrictive and possibly painful. The word is also emphasised by the strong rhyme with 'inch' in line 13.
- The run on between lines 10 and 11 breaks up the flow of the poem. The crisis in the relationship will also soon be resolved.
- The final line shows the ambivalent feelings. 'Fall or fly' implies both excitement and fear at striking out away from maternal care.

### Theme and interpretation
- The central metaphor for this poem is the tape measure connecting mother and son. It stands for the original umbilical cord that connected them and it reappears in the ideas of a kite string and a space walk.
- The mother helping her son to set up his own home represents the point where the umbilical cord must finally break.

### Good matches
- Song of the Old Mother, On My First Sonne, The Affliction of Margaret, Little Boy Lost/Little Boy Found, Before You Were Mine (parent/child links)
- Sonnet 130, Clare's Sonnet, Anne Hathaway (sonnet uses and variations)

## Homecoming – Simon Armitage

Lovers use a trust game to ease a painful memory.

### Setting and context

- Neither character in the poem is identified, but the speaker is probably male and the person addressed female.

### Form and techniques

- Free verse in 4 irregular stanzas, with regular rhythm and use of run-on lines.
- Time is an important factor in the poem. The speaker is addressing a loved one in the present in stanza 1. Stanzas 2 and 3 refer to the past, but in line 15 the future relationship of the 2 lovers is introduced. In stanza 4 the present actions of the lovers recreate, in a new way, the past event.
- The shift in time is strikingly indicated by the idea of a phone call across 16 years. The image suggests that the meeting of the lovers was inevitable.
- The main symbols used are the trust game (a loving relationship) and the yellow jacket (family disharmony). In the final stanza these 2 symbols are combined to represent restored harmony.
- The language in stanza 2 is clichéd – these are familiar situations – and becomes more clipped as tempers get shorter. It ends in the single-word sentence 'Bed.'
- The 'figure' in stanza 3 is not the father – the healing fantasy begins here.
- In the final stanza the speaker becomes the yellow jacket in an attempt to restore the lost harmony through trust.
- The 'fatherly' advice is expressed in imperative verbs. Some instructions, like 'think' in line 1, could be addressed either to the reader or the lover.

### Theme and interpretation

- This is a love poem in which the speaker gives a series of instructions that allow the loved one to relive a traumatic event from the past and take away its pain.
- The idea of a the telephone call that is made 16 years before time implies that the speaker would like to have compensated for the event at the time.
- By 'becoming' the yellow jacket the speaker is able to travel back in time.

### Good matches

- Little Boy Lost/Little Boy Found, The Affliction of Margaret, Before You Were Mine (parent/child relationship)
- Ulysses, Song of the Old Mother, Elvis's Twin Sister (1st person used to explore personality)

## November – Simon Armitage

Two people escort a grandmother to hospital where she is going to die.

### Setting and context

- The person addressed is identified as 'John'. The speaker is presumably male.
- Location is not important, though an unnamed 'famous station' is mentioned.

### Form and techniques

- Regular 3-line stanzas except for the final stanza which has 2 lines. Some use of rhyme.
- The awkwardness of the situation is emphasised by the harsh 'a' sounds in the 1st line.
- Rhyming of 'trinkets' and 'blankets' in stanza 2 emphasises the contrast between the personal world the grandma is leaving and the impersonal one she is entering.
- The closing in of old age and death is underlined by the tightening of the rhyming in the last 5 lines.
- Final 2 lines contrast life and death. The rhythm of line 16 flows, while that of line 17 is halting but emphatic.
- Puns used twice: line 7 'It is time' means 'time to go' and 'the problem is the passage of time'; line 17 'get out ... of this life' means 'exit from this life' and 'gain from this life'. This makes the ending ambiguous.
- Extended imagery in the last part of the poem. References to 'twilight', 'terror of the dusk' and the 'failing' evening all suggest that the day, like a human life, must end.
- Another natural cycle, the year, is evoked by the title of the poem. November is the twilight of the year.
- The 2 men are powerless to stop the passage of time: they too are 'failing' as they watch night come on without doing anything about it.
- Allusion to the TV mystery series 'The Twilight Zone' adds to the idea that the end of life is a descent into the unknown. This idea is reinforced by the reference to the old people as 'monsters'.

### Theme and interpretation

- This poem reminds us that the end of life is as inevitable as the end of the day or the end of the year.
- Our sadness at other people's death is also sadness at the thought of our own mortality.

### Good matches

- Ulysses, Tichborne's Elegy (attitudes to death)
- Tichborne's Elegy, Stealing (despairing tone)

# Simon Armitage

## Those bastards in their mansions – Simon Armitage

An urban guerrilla comments on the inequalities between rich and poor.

### Setting and context

- This is a short *Book of Matches* poem.
- The setting seems to be a historical/mythological mix.
- The historical context is vaguely pre-industrial – suggested by 'britches' and 'torches', 'palaces and castles' – possibly the French Revolution.
- The speaker has committed some sort of (unspecified) crime.

### Form and techniques

- 14-line, sonnet-like format. Irregular rhyming and stanzas but concludes with a couplet. 1st person perspective but clearly not autobiographical.
- Emotive terms used to suggest differences between the rich 'bastards' in their 'mansions', 'palaces' and 'castles' and the 'threadbare' revolutionary.
- Allusion to the myth of Prometheus suggests that the speaker has committed a major offence against the rich.
- Speaker seems to have played an educative role, possibly because he is a poet?
- Use of internal rhymes shows a defiance of convention and a tendency to hide the obvious – as a revolutionary must.

### Theme and interpretation

- The myth of Prometheus is used to give depth to a poem that underlines the differences between rich and poor. Possibly the crime is being a poet.
- The speaker's crime is not specified, but as it is against the rich he gains most readers' sympathy.
- The poem implies that the struggle between rich and poor will always take place and that those who engage in it need to be cautious.
- Ambiguity and mystery adds glamour to the speaker. A specific crime could be disapproved of by some readers.

### Good matches

- The Laboratory, My Last Duchess, Havisham (disliking someone)
- Sonnet 130, Clare's Sonnet, Anne Hathaway (sonnet uses and variations, rhyme, repetition)

---

## Kid – Simon Armitage

An embittered, grown-up Robin reflects on his relationship with Batman.

### Setting and context

- The speaker is a grown-up Robin from the Batman and Robin duo.
- Evidence in the poem suggests that this is the Robin from the 1960s Batman television series staring Adam West as Batman and Burt Ward as Robin.

### Form and techniques

- Dramatic monologue: Robin is the speaker and Batman is the implied listener.
- Single unstressed rhyme throughout – rather like a rap, a form associated with rebellious youth.
- Robin's view is cynical and contrasts with the positive view of Batman and the false views held by the public.
- Robin felt 'ditched' or abandoned, while Batman sees the end of his partnership with Robin as a release into the 'wild blue yonder'.
- Includes British slang terms such as 'sacked' and 'motor' (for car) as well as American colloquialisms – the language deliberately lacks respect.
- 'Holy robin-redbreast-nest-egg-shocker!' is a parody of Robin's speech, as well as of a newspaper headline suggesting some financial impropriety on Batman's part. The following line extends the parody and suggests Robin's negative reaction.
- The pun on 'shadow' in line 20 suggests that Batman is now without a partner and without substance.

### Theme and interpretation

- Batman and Robin (the Boy Wonder) in the comics do not age; this poem undermines the convention to comment on youth and age.
- Armitage imagines a grown-up Robin and uses him to attack the comfortable myths about the relationship between the 2 characters.
- The poem suggests that even super-heroes are only human and that readers should not accept myths at face value.

### Good matches

- The Laboratory, My Last Duchess, Havisham (disliking someone)
- Song of the Old Mother, The Laboratory, Ulysses, My Last Duchess (methods of creating 1st person persona)

GCSE English & Literature: Exam Preparation Support Pack © HarperCollins *Publishers* 2003

# Simon Armitage

## Hitcher – Simon Armitage

A man takes out the frustrations of his job on an unsuspecting hitch-hiker.

### Setting and context

- A contemporary setting and a specific northern location.

### Form and techniques

- 1st person persona, regular 5-line stanzas, some rhyme (mostly internal).
- The internal rhymes in lines 1 and 5 suggest the relentless working world. The lack of rhymes in the rest of the poem shows that the incident is outside the normal order of things.
- The weather imagery associated with the speaker is negative – 'under the weather' at first but improves at the end. The weather imagery associated with the hitcher evokes ideas of freedom (the wind).
- Use of specific details – 'Astra', 'Leeds', 'Harrogate', 'Krooklok' – adds to the realism of the poem and makes the sudden act of violence emerging from ordinary events seem all the more shocking.
- The deadpan tone shows that the speaker is not fully aware of the meaning of his actions. He is as pleased about not swerving as he is about hitting the hitcher. The suggestion is that the pressures of the modern world deaden emotions.

- There are clear links between the driver and the hitcher – they are both the same age and travelling the same road for contrasting reasons.
- The hitcher's use of clichés and his slightly smug tone allow the reader to see why he irritated the driver.
- The phrase 'stitch that' at the end of the poem is sometimes used after a blow in a fight. The speaker is using the language of random aggression but does not seem to appreciate the seriousness of his actions.

### Theme and interpretation

- The poem contrasts freedom and responsibility.
- The speaker attacks the hitcher out of irritation at the contrast between their lives.
- The dead life of the driver is emphasised by his lack of emotional response to his crime.

### Good matches

- The Laboratory, The Man He Killed, My Last Duchess, Education for Leisure (killing)
- Song of the Old Mother, The Laboratory, Ulysses, My Last Duchess (methods of creating 1st person persona)

---

## I've made out a will – Simon Armitage

The speaker leaves most of his body to medical science.

### Setting and context

- A short *Book of Matches* poem.

### Form and techniques

- 14-line, sonnet-like format. Irregular rhyming and stanzas.
- A series of images describe the speaker's body in stanza 1.
- The 'jellies' etc. suggest the softer parts of the human body.
- The 'web of nerves and veins' is the structure that holds the rest together and through which communication takes place.
- The 'loaf of brains' evokes the shape of brains and the expression 'use your loaf'.
- The 'fillings and stitches and wounds' image reminds us that bodies are subject to decay and damage.
- Blood is described as 'a gallon exactly of bilberry soup' to indicate its quantity and its role in 'feeding' the rest of the body.
- The 'chassis or cage or cathedral of bone' suggests strong underlying structures which are nonetheless beautiful.
- The lists of items linked by 'and' suggest the mechanical nature of the body.

- The images in stanzas 2 and 3 are all to do with machines and suggest the body in motion.
- However, a mechanical view of the body does not tie in well with the view of the heart as a centre of emotion: 'but not the heart' at the end of stanza 1 is picked up in stanza 3 and forms the main point of the poem.
- 'Hangs' in the final line suggests both the central position of the heart and the fact that it has stopped.

### Theme and interpretation

- This is a light-hearted look at human frailty.
- The body is seen as either a set of components or as a sort of clock – neither of these things are usually treated with any sentiment.
- The omission of the heart from the donation suggests that there is something more than mere components at our centres.
- The imagery in the poem is commonplace but Armitage suggests that even in the commonplace there is something special.

### Good matches

- Tichborne's Elegy, Ulysses, Education for Leisure (death)
- Sonnet 130, Clare's Sonnet, Anne Hathaway (sonnet uses and variations, rhyme, repetition)

GCSE English & Literature: Exam Preparation Support Pack © HarperCollins *Publishers* 2003

## The Song of the Old Mother – William Butler Yeats

An old woman contrasts her own life with that of young people.

### Setting and context

- The old woman in the poem describes a life of poverty and hard work.
- The reference to the light of the stars implies a rural setting.

### Form and techniques

- Rhyming couplets. Simple rhythm and choice of vocabulary. Mostly monosyllabic words except in lines 6 and 7 describing the young.
- The poem is in 3 sections: the speaker's day; a contrasting description of young people's lives; a reflection on the old woman's life.
- Light imagery is used to describe the old mother: she makes the fire, works even by starlight and tends the embers of the fire at the end of the poem.
- The poem is a single sentence connected by 'and's. This implies that, in the woman's view, one thing leads on to another in a never-ending round of light and dark and that, one day, old age will come to the young.
- The alliteration of 'l' and the internal rhyming of 'young' and 'long' stretch the time it takes to speak line 5 to echo the luxurious and time-wasting nature of young people's lives.

- Youth is associated with the strong light at the middle of the day. The old woman brings the weak fire to life in the morning and contemplates its fading away in the evening. Thus a day is a metaphor for a human life.
- The weakness of her fire is emphasised by alliteration on 'flicker' and 'feeble' and by the use of the word 'glow'.
- There is some bitterness in the old mother's criticism of young girls being obsessed by ribbons and whether their hair is in place. The weak sigh of the young contrasts with the reality and strength of natural forces like the wind.

### Theme and interpretation

- The contrast between youth and age.
- The basic language and the use of nature imagery (fire, stars and wind) gives the poem a universal and timeless appeal.
- The repetition of 'and' implies that youth and age are part of the same endless cycle.

### Good matches

- Digging, Follower, Catrin, Before You Were Mine, Mother, any distance ..., The Affliction of Margaret, My First Sonne, Little Boy Lost/Little Boy Found (adult/child relationships)
- My Last Duchess, The Village Schoolmaster, Inversnaid, Kid, Perch and others (rhyming couplets)

## On My First Sonne – Ben Jonson

A poet reflects on the death of his 7-year-old son.

### Setting and context

- Written in a period when infant mortality was very common.
- Jonson's religious faith is very evident.

### Form and techniques

- Rhyming couplets, mostly end-stopped. Simple rhythm and plain choice of words – generally monosyllables. Polysyllabic words (e.g. 'miserie', 'poetrie') stand out.
- Single stanza of 12 lines. Perhaps a sonnet that wasn't completed?
- Imagery is simple and direct, often evoking Biblical ideas. Jonson's son is the 'child of my right hand', just as Jesus sits on God's right hand. The idea of the son being 'lent' would remind 17th-century readers of the parable of the talents.
- The word 'exacted' is strictly correct in terms of debt collection but reflects an unforgiving attitude on God's part.
- Line 5 breaks the rhythm of the calm opening to the poem. Further attention is drawn to Jonson's distress by the exclamation 'O' and its near rhyme with 'now'. The line has 2 major pauses in it and there is a run-on into line 6.
- Alliteration of 's' in line 7 seems to be an attempt to sooth.

- The monosyllabic final 2 lines are slow and deliberate. The 2-syllable 'never' stands out rather bleakly.

### Theme and interpretation

- The poem needs to be read in its historical context. Adults at that time had to be able to cope with the death of children.
- A modern poem along similar lines would seem rather harsh – the conclusion is not to love later children quite so much.
- Nevertheless Jonson seems not really to be following his own advice. Perhaps he is only trying to find ways of coping with a clearly devastating loss, e.g. one of the sorrows that the child will not face is the death of his own children.
- The comfort about heaven seems conventional rather than felt.

### Good matches

- Mid-Term Break, October, November, Tichborne's Elegy (attitudes towards death)
- The Affliction of Margaret, Follower, Before You Were Mine (1st-person statements)
- My Last Duchess, Inversnaid, Kid, Perch and others (rhyming couplets)

## The Little Boy Lost/The Little Boy Found – William Blake

A boy loses sight of his father in the dark but is miraculously rescued and returned to his mother.

### Setting and context

- Two poems from *Songs of Innocence*, which are addressed to children.
- Almost all aspects of the poems are 'archetypal' (universal) – this could be any boy in any dark and dangerous place.
- The role of the father is ambiguous – he loses the boy but God appears 'like his father' in the 2nd poem.
- down at this point to focus on the boy's isolation.
- 'Led by the wand'ring light' is both naturalistic – these lights are the result of marsh gas – and an allusion to the Bible: in Exodus the Children of Israel are led through the desert by a light provided by God.
- God intervenes – this is acceptable in a poem for children.
- The poem seems to be saying that the ideal father is God. The earthly father lost the boy.
- The word 'weeping' in the final line applies to both the mother and the boy.

### Theme and interpretation

- A child would see the poems as describing a danger faced and overcome.
- Adults might reflect on the role of the parents in the drama. The father is at fault for going too fast and is shown up by the ideal father, God.
- The mother is active in searching for her son, but God is the one who rescues the child.

### Form and techniques

- Both poems use quatrains and abcb rhyme schemes – a simple ballad metre for a simple story.
- The simple structure of the story is calculated to appeal to children.
- A real danger is presented quickly and efficiently, and then the problem is resolved, just as quickly, through divine intervention.

#### Little Boy Lost

- Dialogue is used to make the situation more dramatic.
- The mist disappears after the father is gone, giving the child a clear view of his danger.

#### Little Boy Found

- Alliteration of the letter 'l' in the 1st 2 lines makes them difficult to pronounce and so slows the poem

### Good matches

- Digging, Follower, Catrin, Before You Were Mine, Mother, any distance ..., On My First Sonne, The Affliction of Margaret (parent/child relationships)
- The Song of the Old Mother, Elvis's Twin Sister, Stealing (simple imagery)

---

## The Affliction of Margaret – William Wordsworth

A mother is anxious about the whereabouts of her son.

### Setting and context

- William Wordsworth was from the Lake District, an isolated area which many young people had to leave in order to find work. Margaret's affliction would have been common to many poor people of the era.
- Wordsworth was unusual, at the time, for writing about such problems.

### Form and techniques

- A narrative poem written in simple language in 7-line stanzas with a regular rhythm.
- The regular ababccc rhyme scheme is useful in holding together a comparatively long poem. The triple rhyme at the ends of verses can be very emphatic.
- The poem sets up a mystery that is never resolved. Margaret's son has been away for 7 years. Why has he not contacted her?
- The focus is on her fears and anxieties rather than answering the question.
- Various devices are used to give the impression of a spoken voice, e.g. exclamations (lines 3, 8, 12, 22, 25, 29, 38, 46), questions (lines 2, 7, 14) and repetition (line 55).
- Emphatic alliteration of 'b' in lines 16–17 expresses Margaret's pride and confidence.
- The simple natural imagery used in lines 65–70 expresses how small things disturb Margaret, and gives an idea of how unhappy her ignorance of her son's fate makes her.
- Assonance in the final line emphasises Margaret's isolation.

### Theme and interpretation

- A mother's love for a child.
- Margaret's fears and anxieties are at the centre of the poem.
- She worries that his neglect is due to lack of love for her, but then rejects this most hurtful of possibilities.
- The poem expresses a common anxiety in a particular and powerful way. The reader is meant to feel sympathy for Margaret by the end of the poem.

### Good matches

- Digging, Follower, Catrin, Before You Were Mine, Mother, any distance ..., On My First Sonne, Little Boy Lost/Little Boy Found (parent/child relationships)
- On My First Sonne, Follower, Before You Were Mine (1st-person statements)

GCSE English & Literature: Exam Preparation Support Pack © HarperCollins *Publishers* 2003

- The repetition of 'my foe' and use of the term 'just so' in stanza 3 are the soldier's attempt to convince himself that he has acted correctly.
- In stanza 4 the soldier hesitantly pieces together a life for his enemy. He is beginning to see how close he is, or was, to his enemy.
- The final rhyme is slightly strained. The soldier is not really convinced by his own argument, and the understatement of 'quaint and curious' is further evidence that he is not comfortable with his thoughts.

### Theme and interpretation

- The soldier is a killer, but he has not killed for personal motives.
- The soldier enlisted for economic reasons and does not appear to have thought about the consequences of war until he killed someone.
- He sees the man he killed as similar to himself and clearly finds this thought disturbing.

### Good matches

- My Last Duchess, The Laboratory, Tichborne's Elegy, Education for Leisure, The Hitcher, Mid-Term Break, The Field-Mouse (killing and death)
- My Last Duchess, The Laboratory, Ulysses, Education for Leisure, Kid, The Hitcher, Salome, Elvis's Twin Sister (use of persona)

## The Man He Killed – Thomas Hardy

After a battle, a soldier reflects on the ironies involved in killing someone in a war.

### Setting and context

- Written during the second Boer War (1899–1902) but applies to all wars.

### Form and techniques

- Simple 4-line stanzas with an abab rhyme scheme. The poem centres on the simple fact that in most wars the soldiers who kill each other have no feelings of hatred towards each other.
- The soldier clearly identifies with the man he killed, as the history he invents for him is almost certainly his own history.
- Hardy uses colloquial language to reflect the social status of the soldier but he does not try to reproduce the soldier's pronunciation – as someone like Kipling would do in similar poems.
- The soldier's way of speaking is captured in the tautological phrase 'old ancient'.
- The calm and contemplative mood is disrupted in the 3rd stanza as the soldier struggles to come to terms with what he has done.
- The soldier's pause and repetition of 'because' shows that he has not actually thought about the reasons for killing another human being until this point.

- The pattern for the 1st 3 lines in stanzas 1 and 2 is the same. The 1st 3 lines of stanza 3 begin with 'I'. This reflects a change in perspective from things he owned to things he did (or rather didn't have time for).
- The tone of the poem is bleak, and largely achieved through the use of contrasting images. It constantly repeats the message about his forthcoming death.

### Theme and interpretation

- The poem focuses on the contrast between what might have been and what is.
- The idea of death cutting off all earthly pleasures and possibilities is heavily emphasised.
- Oddly, for a Christian martyr, there are no references to life after death.

### Good matches

- Mid-Term Break, October, November, On My First Sonne (attitudes towards death)
- On My First Sonne, The Affliction of Margaret, Follower, Before You Were Mine (1st-person statements)

## Tichborne's Elegy – Chidiock Tichborne

A young man, on the verge of execution, laments the shortness of his life.

### Setting and context

- Chidiock Tichborne was 28 years old when he wrote this poem, shortly before his execution as a Roman Catholic martyr in 1586.

### Form and techniques

- 6-line stanzas with an ababcc rhyme scheme. The last line is a refrain which gains extra emphasis from being part of a couplet.
- Structure is very similar in all stanzas – this focuses attention on any variations used. E.g. the refrain appears in a slightly altered form in line 16.
- The imagery throughout is simple and based on everyday life, or occasionally the Bible.
- In stanza 1 emphasis is achieved by contrast: youth/cares, joy/pain, corn/tares, good/vain hope of gain.
- The 2nd stanza uses a series of paradoxes: heard/not told etc. These force the reader to think about their meanings. Extra emphasis is gained by the repetition of 'and yet'.
- The 3rd stanza states that opposites – death and the womb, life and being a ghost, and the earth and the tomb – are the same thing for the poet.

## Sonnet 130 – William Shakespeare

A love sonnet which does not praise the object of the poet's affections.

### Setting and context

- This is one of 153 sonnets by Shakespeare dealing with various aspects of love.
- Sonnets in praise of one's lover were a very popular form in the 16th and early 17th centuries, but they were often full of clichés.

### Form and techniques

- This is a standard Shakespearean sonnet with a characteristic ababcdcdefefgg rhyme scheme. The 'point' of the poem is contained in the couplet at the end.
- The main part of the poem runs through a number of clichéd images used in the poetry of the day, each time claiming that the real mistress does not live up to the standard set by such stereotyped comparisons.
- The roses comparison attacks metaphor itself, as Shakespeare states that having seen real roses he cannot find such things in his mistress's cheeks.
- The perfumes comparison is almost insulting with its use of understatement and the implication that his mistress's breath smells.
- The goddess comparison is an example of honesty and common sense just before the punch line about women 'belied with false compare'.

### Theme and interpretation

- The twin concerns of the poem are honesty and language.
- The 1st part of the poem 'admits' that Shakespeare's mistress does not live up to the standards set by poetry.
- The final couplet attacks these standards as lies and false comparisons.
- The reason for these false comparisons is, Shakespeare suggests, a lack of concern for language. Poets are content to use off the shelf expressions that do not reflect reality. Shakespeare himself is careful to record his own observations of reality and, in the goddess comparison, admit the limits of his own experience.
- The mistress in the poem is unlikely to be flattered by it, but the last lines are still a complement to his mistress: they claim that she is rarer than any other woman who has been written about recently.

### Good matches

- Digging, October, Anne Hathaway (writing)
- Anne Hathaway, I've made out a will ..., Patrolling Barnegat, Mali, Perch (imagery)
- Clare's Sonnet, Those bastards ..., I've made out a will ..., Anne Hathaway (sonnet)

---

## Patrolling Barnegat – Walt Whitman

Human beings struggle against a storm.

### Setting and context

- Barnegat is a dangerous area of the sea near New Jersey, USA.

### Form and techniques

- Sonnet form with an octave and a sestet, and a simple rhyme scheme.
- All lines end in verbs in the continuous present tense ('-ing' form), which suggests the power and also the monotony of a storm.
- The octave focuses on the storm. The sestet introduces the human element.
- 'Is', used in the 2 questions in line 9, is the only verb not in the continuous present tense.
- The patrollers are described as 'dim, weird forms', as if their humanity is difficult to discern in the storm.
- The verbs applied to the patrollers are: 'breasting' (the wind), 'advancing', 'wending', 'struggling', 'confronting' and 'warily watching'. They suggest that the patrollers are almost as vigorous as the storm but responding to it rather than active.
- The personification of the storm ('roar', 'muttering', 'savagest trinity', 'demoniac laughter') implies a madhouse.
- Onomatopoeic alliteration in line 6 suggests the sounds of the sands.

### Theme and interpretation

- The principal theme of this poem is the savagery of the storm.
- This is opposed by the wary watchers who are barely visible in its worse moments.
- Nevertheless their unrelenting efforts are necessary to keep the sea safe.

### Good matches

- Clare's Sonnet, Sonnet 130, Those bastards ..., I've made out a will ..., Ann Hathaway (sonnet)
- Storm on the Island, Clare's Sonnet, Blackberry-Picking, October (nature)
- Anne Hathaway, I've made out a will ..., Mali, Perch (imagery)

GCSE English & Literature: Exam Preparation Support Pack © HarperCollins *Publishers* 2003

## My Last Duchess – Robert Browning

A wealthy Duke describes how he had his previous wife killed for being too easily pleased.

### Setting and context

- The aristocratic setting is established by the title.
- The Renaissance period is established by the location (Ferrara) and the artists referred to (Frà Pandolf and Claus of Innsbruck – invented by Browning).
- The Duke's power and influence is shown by the fact that he can have his wife killed with no consequences for himself.

### Form and techniques

- Dramatic monologue: the speaker is the Duke of Ferrara, the implied listener the ambassador negotiating the Duke's next marriage.
- Rhyming couplets used throughout, but this normally powerful form is overridden by the use of run-ons. This reflects the personality of the Duke who overrides normal rules of behaviour.
- The too easily pleased Duchess has now been reduced to a portrait.
- The Duke controls access to the portrait, whearas he couldn't control his wife.
- The Duchess is associated with natural things – warm heart, sunset, cherry bough, blushing cheeks. The Duke is associated with 'dead' things – portrait, statue, his 'nine-hundred-years-old name'.
- Heavy emphasis on the 'oo' sound when the Duke chooses 'never to stoop' (line 43).
- The Duke shows some sense of shame when he uses a euphemism to describe the killing of his wife.
- The Duke's revelations are shocking enough, but the fact that they are being made to a man who has come to negotiate on a new marriage emphasises his arrogance and pride.

### Theme and interpretation

- A portrait of power and prestige in a bygone age.
- The Duke is so secure in his social, financial and political world that he can talk matter-of-factly about the killing of his wife.
- As a psychological type the Duke represents the male desire to control women.
- From a Victorian point of view the Duchess's fate presents a bleak image of the powerlessness of women.

### Good matches

- Hitcher, Stealing, Education for Leisure, The Laboratory, Havisham (disturbing characters)
- Hitcher, Stealing, Education for Leisure, The Laboratory, Ulysses, Havisham, Elvis's Twin Sister (use of persona/dramatic monologue)

## The Laboratory – Robert Browning

A wealthy woman visits a laboratory to purchase a poison with which to kill a rival.

### Setting and context

- The aristocratic setting is established by reference to 'dance at the Kings'.
- Set in pre-revolutionary France – the 'ancien régime'.
- The laboratory, and the old man who works there, belong at the opposite end of the social spectrum from the speaker.
- Interesting that a male poet has assumed a female persona.

### Form and techniques

- Dramatic monologue. The speaker is an unidentified member of the aristocracy, the implied listener the chemist preparing the potion.
- Rhyming couplets in quatrains used throughout – most lines are end stopped, emphasising the rhyme.
- Strong, dactylic rhythm in places, e.g. line 25. This makes the poem lively and immediate and tends, with the strong rhyme, to undermine its seriousness.
- The speaker is obsessed with appearance – the beautiful potions, the physical features of her rivals, her own stature.
- The ability to kill her rival gives the speaker an unaccustomed taste of power – she fantasises about killing other rivals with poison.
- The speaker looks forward to the death of her rival and hopes to enjoy it – perhaps out of cruelty or desire for revenge.
- At the end of the poem the speaker allows the old chemist to kiss her. This shows how far she is prepared to go to gain her revenge.

### Theme and interpretation

- Another Victorian portrait of the powerlessness of women, but this time fighting back.
- Unlike the Duke, the speaker has to operate in secret. She also has to arrange the killing herself.
- However, she has to seek the help of a man to carry out her scheme.
- Of all the killers in the Anthology this speaker has the strongest motivation.

### Good matches

- Hitcher, Stealing, Education for Leisure, The Laboratory, Havisham (disturbing characters)
- Hitcher, Stealing, Education for Leisure, The Laboratory, Ulysses, Havisham, Elvis's Twin Sister (use of persona/dramatic monologue)

## The Village Schoolmaster – Oliver Goldsmith

A description of an admired (and feared) local character.

### Setting and context

- The poem is an extract from *The Deserted Village*, which describes the depopulation of the countryside in the later 18th century.
- There is therefore a sense in the poem that such men as the schoolmaster are no longer around. The poem is all in the past tense.

### Form and techniques

- Rhyming couplets are used throughout the poem and there is a steady rhythm, reflecting the controlled and calm environment created by the schoolmaster.
- The schoolmaster was clearly a major character in village life but the small size of his school tells us that he would not have been so important in the wider world.
- The portrait shows that the schoolmaster had good discipline in the probably rather rough and ready world of the village school.
- The harshness of his discipline is excused by the schoolmaster's love of learning.
- In the wider world of the village the schoolmaster is admired for his education, even though the villagers do not necessarily understand him.
- Some of Goldsmith's vocabulary is 'mock heroic'. Words and phrases like 'boding tremblers', 'counterfeited glee', 'dismal tidings' and 'vanquished' give the schoolmaster far more dignity than he would have commanded in reality.
- The extract comes to a rousing conclusion in lines 21–3, as the schoolmaster's intellectual conflicts with the parson are described in suitably overblown and bombastic terms.
- This is followed by the emphatic, almost monosyllabic, final line.

### Theme and interpretation

- The schoolmaster is meant to be admired as a type who is no longer to be found in the countryside.
- His discipline is harsh but he loved learning.
- His learning was admired but only by people who were ignorant themselves. However, it is not up to the standard of the only other educated person in village, the parson.
- This is a far from idealised portrait, as the language emphasises his pompousness.

### Good matches

- My father thought it bloody queer ..., Digging, Ulysses (admiration)
- My Last Duchess, Inversnaid, Kid, Perch (rhyming couplets)

---

## Ulysses – Alfred Tennyson

A mythical adventurer contemplates old age and resolves not to let it beat him.

### Setting and context

- Ulysses has returned home, after 20 years of war and travel abroad, to his rough and rocky kingdom of Ithaca.
- Ulysses' adventures are the subject of Homer's epic poem *The Odyssey*, which would have been well known to any educated reader in the 19th century.
- Tennyson mentions some of his adventures in the course of the poem, both to establish Ulysses' character and to remind readers of his story.
- Tennyson said that 'Ulysses' was a response to the death of his friend Arthur Hallam.

### Form and techniques

- Dramatic monologue in blank verse. The 1st part is a soliloquy, but the implied listeners to the final part are Ulysses' mariner companions.
- Emphatic iambic rhythms mark key moments in the text:

*That hoard, and sleep, and feed,*
*and know not me.* (line 5)
*To strive, to seek, to find,*
*and not to yield.* (line 70)

Line 5, which emphasises Ulysses' frustration, peters out with the equal stresses of 'know not me'. Line 70 emphasises his determination: the strong rhythm continues to the end and the 'not' is strongly stressed.

- The poem has the following sections: frustration at his present situation (stanza 1); nostalgia for his adventurous past (stanza 2); a contrast between himself and his son (stanza 3); a resolution to go on one last adventure (stanza 4).

### Theme and interpretation

- Past pleasures are important but we should not dwell on them too much. Instead, we should look forward and face the future with determination.
- Key images include: hatred of idleness ('idle king', 'rust unburnished'); enjoyment of life ('drink life to the lees', 'roaming with a hungry heart'); the place of duty ('decent not to fail'); and determination to carry on ('my purpose holds to sail beyond the sunset', 'to strive, to seek, to find ...').

### Good matches

- Kid, Elvis's Twin Sister, Salome, Anne Hathaway, Havisham, My Last Duchess (fictional and historical characters)
- Stealing, Education for Leisure, The Laboratory, Havisham, Elvis's Twin Sister (dramatic monologue)

## Inversnaid – Gerard Manley Hopkins

A description of a wild Scottish burn (stream).

### Setting and context

- Inversnaid is a hamlet on the eastern shore of Loch Lomond. The rock pools and waterfalls of the Snaid Burn are the subject of the poem.
- Gerard Manley Hopkins believed that poetry should try to capture the inner as well as the outer landscape. The inner landscape, or 'inscape', is what makes a scene unique and individual.

### Form and techniques

- The poem is written in rhyming couplets and divided into quatrains.
- It makes extensive use of alliteration as a structuring device. All lines contain at least 1 pair of alliterated words, with 3 words in line 1 and extensive alliteration of 'l' and 'w' in the final stanza.
- The total effect of the consistent rhyme and alliteration is to create a highly patterned 'soundscape' which reflects the complexity and wildness of the stream being described.
- The poem begins with a rush of sounds and images related to the fast moving stage of the burn's progress. By the time the burn flows into the pool (stanza 2) the sound effects are less obvious and the flow of the sentences stops in line 8.

- The 3rd stanza describes a landscape that has been created by the action of streams such as the burn. Phrases such as 'wiry heathpacks' show that he saw even this landscape as active.
- Hopkins's concern for the uniqueness of the 'inscape' he has described is emphasised by the repetition in the 4th stanza.
- As Inversnaid is in Scotland, it is natural for Hopkins to use Scottish vocabulary.
- He also invents words, making up combinations such as 'rollrock', all to fit into his 'soundscape'.

### Theme and interpretation

- Beneath the vivid description of a particular stream, Hopkins is saying that the natural landscape is dynamic and possesses its own inner beauty.
- The uniqueness of all landscapes should be preserved.

### Good matches

- Patrolling Barnegat, Storm on the Island, October (nature)
- Digging, Stealing, Patrolling Barnegat, The Eagle (imagery)

## The Eagle – Alfred Tennyson

A simple poem describing a powerful creature in its natural setting.

### Setting and context

- The eagle is described in an isolated setting; its height above the world emphasises its power.
- The thunderbolt is an attribute of Zeus, the king of the Greek gods.

### Form and techniques

- A short intense poem with an emphatic aaa bbb rhyme scheme.
- 'Crookèd hands' humanises the eagle. Likewise, 'mountain walls' suggests he is in his fortress.
- 'Ring'd with the azure world' suggests that the world rotates around the eagle.
- The mighty ocean is reduced to a rumpled sheet.
- There is a loneliness in the eagle's grandeur. The mountain walls keep things out but they also isolate.
- There may be some ambiguity in the word 'falls' at the end – note that a king falls from power.
- Good use of alliteration, e.g. harsh 'c' sounds in line 1, and long 'l' sounds in 'lonely lands' (line 2).
- Assonance adds to the soundscape in 'azure world' and 'sea beneath'.
- Last line has no commas – it has to be read rapidly like the eagle's descent.

### Theme and interpretation

- The poem is a description of an eagle, but it is also a reflection on the loneliness of power. The eagle has long been a symbol of power.
- The isolation would not be a problem for a real eagle but Tennyson humanises this one by giving it hands and placing it in a mountain fortress.
- The eagle's power is also emphasised by the use of the word 'thunderbolt' in the last line. However, thunderbolts only fall, they do not rise again.

### Good matches

- Inversnaid, Patrolling Barnegat, Clare's Sonnet, Storm on the Island, Perch, The Field-Mouse (nature)
- Catrin, Digging, Inversnaid, Clare's Sonnet (imagery)

## Sonnet – John Clare

A simple attempt to capture the peace and tranquillity of an English summer.

### Setting and context

- This poem says what Clare himself likes about summer. Such an intensely personal point of view was a new aspect of poetry when the poem was written.
- Clare's sonnet describes a particular time and place; compare the almost abstract landscape in Blake's 2 poems.

### Form and techniques

- Some sonnets use rhyme to emphasise different parts. Clare's sonnet uses rhyming couplets as if he valued all aspects of the scene equally.
- The description is dynamic – moving from one place to another in the landscape and occasionally focussing on some small detail.
- 'Happy wings' is an example of a 'transferred epithet'. Happy refers to the insects but is actually applied to their wings. This device is often striking and can express ideas very economically.
- The mood of the poem is tranquil but there is a suggestion that it represents only a passing moment – the clouds have just moved away, the wind is shaking the grass and the scene will change.
- The steady rhythm also reflects the peaceful mood of the description.
- Alliteration is used for a number of specific effects. The alliteration of 'w' in line 5 gives the impression of the writer savouring the scene in front of him. The 'b's at the end

of the poem express a sense of delight and excitement.

- The simile in line 6 connects the light summer wind to the more powerful winds of autumn and reflects the transitory nature of summer pleasures. The 's' and 'w' sounds are also onomatopoeic.
- There are no punctuation marks in the poem, giving a sense of an immediate experience.

### Theme and interpretation

- Clare's dynamic description reflects both the activity typical of a summer's day and the fact that all pleasures are transitory.
- The description shifts from place to place and sees movement everywhere. Even the willow tree is not passive but is 'leaning' over the water.
- The description is also inclusive, mentioning flowers, trees, birds and insects as well as the more static parts of the landscape.
- The poem constantly repeats that these are the things that Clare loves. It is not just a picture but a statement of the poet's emotional state.

### Good matches

- Blackberry-Picking, Death of a Naturalist, The Field-Mouse, October, A Difficult Birth, Patrolling Barnegat, Inversnaid (nature and personal responses to nature)
- Sonnet 130, Those bastards ..., I've made out a will ..., Anne Hathaway (sonnet)

### English Literature: poetry: Duffy/Armitage

p186 ⇨

This is the response to the essay question that you assessed on page 186 of the Student's Book. It was awarded a grade D. The annotations on the right show why the extract was awarded a D, and how you could turn it into a grade C. Words in bold are quoted from the examiner's assessment criteria.

---

D grade: **structured comments on similarities or differences.**

To turn this into a grade C, you need to draw out more detail in the similarities and differences. For example:

*Although "Ulysses" and "Tichborne's Elegy" are both about their own deaths, the former is much more positive because the speaker is not giving in, whereas in the latter poem the speaker is accepting death and pondering on what he will miss from life.*

This would fulfil the C grade criterion **sustained focus on similarities/differences.**

---

D grade: **explained response to character/situation/ideas.**

To turn this into a grade C, you need to use a connective to introduce the comparison, and quote from the text to prove your points. For example:

*Death in "Elegy" is about missing out on the "prime of youth", "the feast", "the crop", whereas the speaker in "Education for Leisure" only sees death as an escape from a dull life through an unnecessary killing.*

This would fulfil the C grade criterion **sustained response to situations or ideas.**

---

D grade: **awareness of feeling(s), attitude(s) and ideas.**

To turn this into a grade C, you could explain what role the final line plays in affecting John's outlook on life. For example:

*Although Armitage writes about the pain that death brings, John's reflective comment in the last line shows that life is for the living, and therefore we must all aim to get as much as we can out of life.*

This would fulfil the C grade criterion **appropriate comment on meaning/style.**

---

The main thing about attitudes to death in "November", "Education for Leisure", "Ulysses" and "Tichborne's Elegy" is that two of the speakers are thinking about their own deaths ("Ulysses" and "Tichborne's Elegy") whilst two of them are concerned with the death of others. ("November" and "Education for Leisure"). Another difference is that the speaker in "Education for Leisure" is thinking about causing death. The most positive of the poems is "Ulysses" with its decision to:

strive, to seek, to find and not to yield

The most negative is "Tichborne's Elegy" which just goes on about the shortness of life. The speaker in "Education for Leisure" sees death as a way of getting power and enjoyment out of a dull life.

In "November" John takes his grandma to a home and leaves her there to die. The poem talks about how upsetting this is, but also how it has a positive effect on John and his outlook on life. The most positive poem is "Ulysses" because although the speaker realises he is coming to the end of his life, he battles on and will not give in.

In "Ulysses", the speaker knows he is old and that he should slow down "How dull it is to pause" but he still wants to get on with his life instead of letting his life pass him by and accepting death like in "November".

English Literature: poetry: Duffy/Armitage

---

This is the response to the essay question that you assessed on page 187 of the Student's Book. It was awarded a grade C. The annotations on the right show why the extract was awarded a C, and how you could turn it into a grade B. Words in bold are quoted from the examiner's assessment criteria.

---

C grade: **appropriate comment on meaning/style.**

To turn this into a B grade, you need to develop the point by showing how the poet's language and style create this effect for the reader. For example:

*The use of single-syllable words further creates the pounding idea of the fist upon the table and represents the determination not to give in.*

This would fulfil the B grade criterion **features of language interest explored.**

---

C grade: **explanation of how effects are achieved.**

To turn this into a grade B, you need to explore what we learn from the messages in the poem. For example:

*The repetition of "we" seems to emphasise the idea that we are involved in this death too, not just by bringing grandma but also by being mortal ourselves. This message is reinforced at the end of the poem: "we have to get, John, out of this life".*

This would fulfil the B grade criterion **measured/qualified/exploratory response to writer's ideas and/or methods.**

---

C grade: **effective use of details to support answer.**

To turn this into a grade B, you need to think about what message the writer may want us to take from the poem. For example:

*The poet is saying that if we make the most of opportunities early on in life we will form the habit of positive thinking that will last well into old age.*

This would fulfil the B grade criterion **details linked to writer's intentions and purposes.**

---

You can tell that Ulysses is not going to give up because of the way he expresses his plans:

To strive, to seek, to find and not to yield

The rhythm of this is like he is banging his fist on the table with each point. In "Tichborne's Elegy" the repetition of

And now I live and now my day is done

makes the whole poem sound mournful and makes the process of death seem sort of inevitable. The rhythm of the line is as regular as Tennyson's but it is not as strong because it doesn't repeat anything like the 'to' of "Ulysses". Instead it repeats 'and now' as if death followed on naturally from life and there is nothing we can do about it.

This same idea is expressed in "November" by the simple but effective statement about the impending death of the Grandma, "We have brought her here to die and we know it". The matter of fact statement gives the feeling of being very final. "We know it"

The speaker in "Ulysses" presents death in a negative way "eternal silence", "gloom" and "Death closes all" which signal the end as depressing. However, despite this, the speaker looks forward to the rest of his life in a positive way "for my purpose holds / To sail ... until I die" because he is "Strong in will / To strive ... not to yield". The reason for this positive attitude comes from the speaker's earlier active life. He is used to travelling, meeting others and accepting challenges.

---

This is the response to the essay question that you assessed on pages 189–190 of the Student's Book. It was awarded a grade D. The annotations on the right show why the extract was awarded a D, and how you could turn it into a grade C. Words in bold are quoted from the examiner's assessment criteria.

"Hitcher" by Simon Armitage, "Education for Leisure" by Carol Ann Duffy, "My Last Duchess" and "The Laboratory" by Robert Browning all deal with the theme of murder. All four of the poets have chosen to write from the point of view of the killer and in doing so they seem to want to give the reader some insight into the killer's mind. Probably the strangest murder is the one described in "My Last Duchess" as the Duke seems to have had his wife murdered simply for smiling too much. The most chilling murder is probably the one that is about to take place in "Education for Leisure". In this poem the murderer wants to kill just to make himself feel big. The murder in "Hitcher" is sort of understandable, because the speaker has got a horrible life and the Hitcher's life is free and easy – though killing somebody for this reason is hardly right! The woman in "The Laboratory" seems to have the strongest reason for wanting to kill as her lover is being unfaithful to her.

The four killers are all very different. The two poems by Browning show rich people whereas the killer in "Hitcher" is just about holding onto his job and the one in "Education for Leisure" is unemployed. In terms of why they kill, the Duke and the unemployed person seem to be the most similar. They kill or want to kill not because they hate the other person but because they want to say something about themselves. The Duke can't stand the thought of his wife not respecting his nine-hundred-years-old' name and the unemployed person wants everyone to realise that he is a genius. At least the driver of the car is provoked by the contrast between his life and the hitcher's and he seems to be acting out of a fit of jealousy. The woman in "The Laboratory" is also motivated

**D grade: awareness of feeling(s) and attitude(s).**

To turn this into a C grade, you need to make an appropriate comment on the meaning or style to back up your point. For example:

*This is achieved by the murderer killing less important creatures such as the fly and goldfish earlier in the poem. This suggests that the murder implied at the end of the poem is in the same class.*

This would fulfil the C grade criterion **appropriate comment on meaning/style.**

**D grade: some focus on the task.**

To turn this into a grade C, you need to expand on the point made by referring to the poems in greater detail. For example:

*Both the Duke and the unemployed person want more attention and control. This is revealed when the Duke states, "I gave commands", and by the "panicking" reaction of the budgie in "Education for Leisure" when the goldfish is poured down the toilet.*

This would fulfil the C grade criterion **structured response to task.**

continued ...

## English Literature: poetry: Duffy/Armitage

D grade: **identification of effects intended/achieved.**

To turn this into a grade C, you need to explain how the poet makes the Duke appear cold and calculating. For example:

*The Duke was too proud to tell his wife off for her behaviour ("I choose never to stoop"), and his coldness is shown in the stark "I gave commands; then all smiles stopped together".*

This would fulfil the C grade criterion **explanation of how effects are achieved.**

by jealousy of the woman who has taken her man. The main difference between these two is that the driver acts in a fit of anger whilst the woman plans her murder and goes to the poisoner for help to carry it out. Like the person in "Education for Leisure" she is quite excited by the power that killing someone gives and she even imagines killing off some of her other rivals at court.

The reader gains some understanding of the reasons for murder in all of the poems. The Duke is so powerful that he can boast about his killing to someone who has come to arrange his next marriage, and he appears to be a cold and calculating person who was too proud even to tell his wife off for her behaviour. The woman wanting to kill her rival in love is also quite easy to understand. The two modern killers are more puzzling – why does the driver react so violently and why does the unemployed person need to kill to make himself feel good? Neither Simon Armitage nor Gillian Clarke offer obvious answers to these questions and it is left up to the reader to decide.

GCSE English & Literature: Exam Preparation Support Pack © HarperCollins *Publishers* 2003

# Boost your grade: from B to A

### English Literature: poetry: Heaney/Clarke

This is the response to the essay question that you assessed on page 196 of the Student's Book. It was awarded a grade B. The annotations on the right show why the extract was awarded a B, and how you could turn it into a grade A. Words in bold are quoted from the examiner's assessment criteria.

The "Field Mouse", "Storm on the Island", "Patrolling Barnegat" and "Sonnet" all include descriptions of nature and all four poems use these descriptions as a means of commenting on human life and attitudes. "Storm on the Island" and "Patrolling Barnegat" use the power of the storm to comment on the weakness and insignificance of humanity. "The Field Mouse" and "Sonnet" are both set in the summer but one focuses on happiness whilst the other comments on death and war.

"Storm on the Island" is written from the point of view of an islander and at first attempts to seem unconcerned by the storm saying that 'we are prepared' and 'there are no stacks or stoops that can be lost. But as the poem progresses the fear of the storm becomes more explicit. The absence of trees is an advantage because they will not make a disturbing noise. The sound of the sea, which is normally a comforting background noise,

spits like a tame cat
Turned savage.

Finally the speaker admits that sitting through a storm is like being in a war zone as the wind 'dives and strafes', space is 'a salvo' and the inhabitants are 'bombarded'. These military images suggest the violence of the storm as well as the powerlessness of the victims. The final line of the poem could be defiant or, with its reference to fearing a 'huge nothing', it might be reference to people's fear of death.

---

B grade: **details linked to writer's intentions and purposes.**

To turn this into a grade A, you need to explain why the writer has used a particular image, and what its effect is upon the reader. For example:

*By using this simile Heaney reveals the dual nature of the weather, which can be as harmless as a tame cat, but the next minute turn into a destructive savage creature.*

This would fulfil the A grade criterion **sensitive insight into writer's methods, purposes and characteristics.**

---

B grade: **features of language interest explored.**

To turn this into an A grade, you need to develop the comment further by analysing the effect of the language used. For example:

*The wind "diving" imitates a fighter plane diving before firing on its victims beneath, and "strafes invisibly" implies an attack, made all the more fearful by the fact that you cannot see it approaching.*

This would fulfil the A grade criterion **analysis of writer's use of language and effect(s) on readers.**

continued ...

GCSE English & Literature: Exam Preparation Support Pack © HarperCollins *Publishers* 2003

B grade: **features of language interest explored.**

To turn this into a grade A, you need to develop your comment and analysis of the poet's choice of vocabulary. For example:

*"Struggling" and "confronting" both describe the reactions of the patrollers in the continuous present tense. This emphasises the almost ceaseless battle that they have against the power of the storm, and perhaps the continuous nature of man's struggle against the elements.*

This would fulfil the A grade criterion **analysis of writer's use of language and effect(s) on readers.**

"Patrolling Barnegat" also emphasises the power and energy of the storm. Its power and energy is suggested by the fact that every line ends with a verb in the present continuous tense and sounds are suggested by a great deal of insistent alliteration. The hissing of the snow, for instance being suggested by the 's' sounds of

On beachy slush and sand spirts of snow fierce slanting

The storm with its 'demonic laughter' seems to have its own personality, but the human world is dim and indistinct

(That in the distance! is that a wreck? is the red signal flaring?)

and the human figures are described as 'struggling', 'weird' forms rather than as people as if there was no place for the patrollers in such a fierce place.

The energy of these two poems is in strong contrast to Gillian Clarke's description of a typical summer event on a farm. The hay is being cut by a tractor that looks like it is sailing on a sea as the 'waves' of hay break in front of it. A neighbour's work fills the air with a 'gift of sweetness'. However the scene is far from tranquil. 'The air hums with jets' and there is 'terrible news' on the radio and the speakers children are unable to deal with the field-mouse and the haymaking produces a wave of refugees. The speaker is reminded of the refugees elsewhere in Europe and dreams of her children suffering like the field mouse in the event of civil war. Unlike the first two poems "The field-Mouse" uses nature as a contrasting background for the major concerns of the poem.

English Literature: poetry: pre–1914 poems

p197 ⟹

**A grade: analysis of writer's use of language and effect(s) on readers.**

To turn this into a grade A*, you need to build on your analysis of key words and images to show how they create the specific effects. For example:

"Beaming" not only suggests that the sun is shining brightly, but also hints at a personification of the sun smiling broadly on the world, and making people smile with happiness in response. "White wool sack clouds" creates a pure image which adds to the innocence and tranquillity of the scene.

This would fulfil the A* grade criterion **close textual evaluation or analysis.**

**A grade: insight into structure and significance of patterns of detail.**

To turn this into an A* grade, you could develop the point by giving your own interpretation of the form of the poem. For example:

Clare seems almost as though he is in love with the image he has created. The form of the poem is therefore fitting to complement this feeling because the poet uses the traditional form of a love sonnet, with the repetition/refrain of "I love".

This would fulfil the A* grade criterion **independent discovery and interpretation of significant details.**

**A grade: insight into structure and significance of patterns of detail.**

To turn this into a grade A*, you need to expand on the point made by discussing or evaluating the text in even greater detail. For example:

The piled up alliteration in line 6 emphasises the sound of moving through the "beachy slush", but the choice of the repeated "s" also has the effect of slowing down the line, which emphasises the difficulty of moving through this landscape and weather.

This would fulfil the A* grade criterion **close textual evaluation or analysis.**

This is the response to the essay question that you assessed on page 197 of the Student's Book. It was awarded a grade A. The annotations on the right show why the extract was awarded an A, and how you could turn it into a grade A*. Words in bold are quoted from the examiner's assessment criteria.

John Clare's poem is most interested in nature itself. He tries to capture the beauty of nature by describing the things he loves or likes. There is nothing remarkable about his choices, such as sunshine, fleecy clouds or quiet Moor Hens but as the poem progresses the reader builds up a picture of a tranquil English country scene. The poem is full of enthusiasm and quiet joy: the sun is 'beaming'; the flowers stain their surroundings with 'gold'; the lake is 'clear'; the insects fly on 'happy' wings and both the day and the beetles are 'bright'. The portrait also includes movement so that clouds are 'sailing to the north'; the Moor Hen 'pushes and seeks'; the 'reed clumps rustle' alliteratively in the wind; the willow leans over its lake; the heads of the hay grass 'swing to the summer winds' and the beetles 'play' in the lake. All of this detail is contained in the fourteen lines of the sonnet.

Walt Whitman's sonnet "Patrolling Barnegat" also seems mostly interested in nature itself, but unlike Clare's poem this is nature at its most powerful and violent. Rather than the traditional rhyme scheme of a sonnet Whitman ends every line with a verb, emphasising the ceaseless activity of the storm. The poem begins as it means to go on with the use of the word 'wild' twice and Whitman also uses a number of alliterative effects for emphasis or to suggest the sounds of the storm.

'Shouts of demoniac laughter, fitfully piercing and pealing' for instance gives some idea of the power of and strength of the sounds, whereas the description of the waves' 'combs careering' suggest the speed and harshness of their movement – Whitman also repeats this description to show that the waves continually move. Amongst all of this energy of 'waves, air and midnight' the human figures are 'dim weird forms' that struggle through the night 'warily watching' the storm.

# Boost your grade: from B to A

**English Literature: poetry: pre–1914 poems**

pp199–200 ⇨

This is the response to the essay question that you assessed on pages 199–200 of the Student's Book. It was awarded a grade B. The annotations on the right show why the extract was awarded a B, and how you could turn it into a grade A. Words in bold are quoted from the examiner's assessment criteria.

B grade: **details linked to writer's intentions and purposes.**

To turn this into a grade A, you need to expand on the point made and show how the feature has the specific effects you mention. For example:

*Because the refrain is repeated in every stanza, it acts as a constant reminder that the man's life is about to end, almost like a tolling bell. The effect of this rings in our ears well after the end of the poem – the premature end of his life, and the shortness of all our lives, is the overwhelming thought that we are left with.*

This would fulfil the A grade criterion **insight into structure and significance of patterns of detail.**

B grade: **features of language interest explored.**

To turn this into an A grade, you need to focus more closely on the specific words used and their effect. For example:

*The imagery of food is cleverly used, as the dish of pain replaces the plentiful feast – as if the man's life is cut off at the height of his youth. This makes the reader see the futility of that life.*

This would fulfil the A grade criterion **analysis of writer's use of language and effect(s) on readers.**

"Tichborne's Elegy" and "On My First Sonne", both deal with the subject of death and therefore might be considered depressing by all but the most morbid of readers. "Tichborne's Elegy" is unusual in that it is a meditation on the imminent death of the poet; "On My First Sonne" is a reflection on the death of the poet's first-born child. Both poets respond deeply to these depressing events and in doing so they say things that are not necessarily depressing to the reader.

"Tichborne's Elegy" is almost certainly the more negative of the two poems. This is not surprising as very few people are likely to feel cheerful when they know they are shortly to be executed, but Tichborne makes his Elegy even more depressing by using a mournful refrain at the end of each stanza:

And now I live and now my life is done.

In the first part of the poem, Tichborne treats his life like a calculation and carefully cancels out all its positives with negatives:

My prime of youth is but a frost of cares,
My feast of joy is but a dish of pain

As well as this 'zero sum' Tichborne introduces images that speak of loss or lack of completion in terms of sunless days, unheard tales or fruit fallen before its time. Eventually the effect becomes overwhelming and you are either moved to pity Tichborne or inclined to tell him to stop complaining. What is surprising in this poem by a Christian martyr is that Tichborne does not look beyond death to his heavenly reward.

continued ...

**50**

# Boost your grade: from B to A (cont.)

English Literature: poetry: pre-1914 poems

pp199–200 ⇨

B grade: **developed comparison/contrast of style/ideas/form.**

To turn this into a grade A, you need to bring out the comparison/contrast in greater detail and add your own evaluation. For example:

*Whereas Tichborne's relentless focus on the end of his life seems to have no room for the traditional comforts of Christianity, Jonson does take some comfort from his faith. This makes it a less depressing, more reasonable poem, although not quite as effective for this reason.*

This would fulfil the A grade criterion **evaluative comparison and contrast.**

It is difficult to imagine a more depressing subject than a parent thinking about the death of his child but Ben Jonson's poem "On My First Sonne" is actually much more positive than "Tichborne's Elegy". This is partly because Jonson does take some comfort from his Christian faith and imagines his son as having escaped from the worlds and the fleshes rage,

And if no other misery yet age.

The other factor that prevents the poem from being depressing is the genuine love and tenderness that Jonson expresses in the simple dignified language of the poem. The son of his 'right hand' is something precious that has been 'lent' to him and that he has been forced to pay back, and the poet and playwright sees the boy as his best piece of poetrie.

Jonson is of course sad at the death of his son but he blames himself for loving the boy too well. Not growing too fond of small children was a sensible precaution in the seventeenth century when infant mortality rates were very high but Jonson's final resolution not to love so strongly again leaves the reader feeling saddened on the poet's behalf.

GCSE English & Literature: Exam Preparation Support Pack © HarperCollins *Publishers* 2003

## About the author

John Steinbeck was born in Salinas, California, in 1902. After attending Stanford University without graduating he moved to New York in 1925. He tried to become a freelance writer there but eventually returned to California. His first successful book was *Tortilla Flat* (1935), a series of humorous stories about poor people in Monterey, California. *Of Mice and Men* was published in 1937; like his most famous novel, *The Grapes of Wrath* (1939), it tells the story of dispossessed migrant workers. John Steinbeck died in New York City in 1968.

## Historical setting

*Of Mice and Men* is set in the decade before the Second World War when economic depression gripped America. The characters in *Of Mice and Men* belong to a rather old-fashioned group of workers whose lifestyle was slowly disappearing under the economic pressures of the 1930s. Steinbeck does not regret this as he shows how grim, unrewarding and, above all, lonely the life of such migrant workers could be. George and Lennie have difficulty in finding work: the novel begins in Soledad, but their previous job was in the mining town of Weed at the other end of California.

**Migrant workers.** Almost all agricultural work is seasonal, demanding large amounts of labour at some times of the year and virtually none at others. The labour-intensive work was often done by bands of men travelling around the country as demands shifted from farm to farm and crop to crop. During the depression thousands of workers travelled west to California from areas afflicted by drought in other parts of America.

**Mechanisation.** After the First World War lower agricultural prices severely affected farmers in America. This development led to larger farms, more machinery to run them, greater debt for the farmers and fewer jobs for seasonal and migrant workers.

**The Dust Bowl.** Economic pressures on farmers forced them to cultivate more and more land. This, combined with wind erosion, eventually exhausted the soil in many of the Great Plains states, such as Oklahoma, Texas and Kansas. The ruined agricultural workers in this 'Dust Bowl' saw California as a rich and fertile land of hope and added their numbers to those looking for work there.

**The Wall Street Crash.** The stock market crash of 1929 made matters worse for farmers. Banks refused to lend money for mortgages and farmers lost their property and means of livelihood. They were forced to go on the road to find work at a time when unemployment was approaching 25 percent.

**The American Dream.** George and Lennie's dream of a better life on their own farm was shared by many at this time; both by those that had never owned farms and by those who had lost them. In a larger sense George and Lennie's dream represents the quest for a better life, the American Dream. The American Constitution guarantees each citizen the right to 'life, liberty and the pursuit of happiness' but, as the novel shows, the pursuit of happiness will not necessarily bring happiness itself.

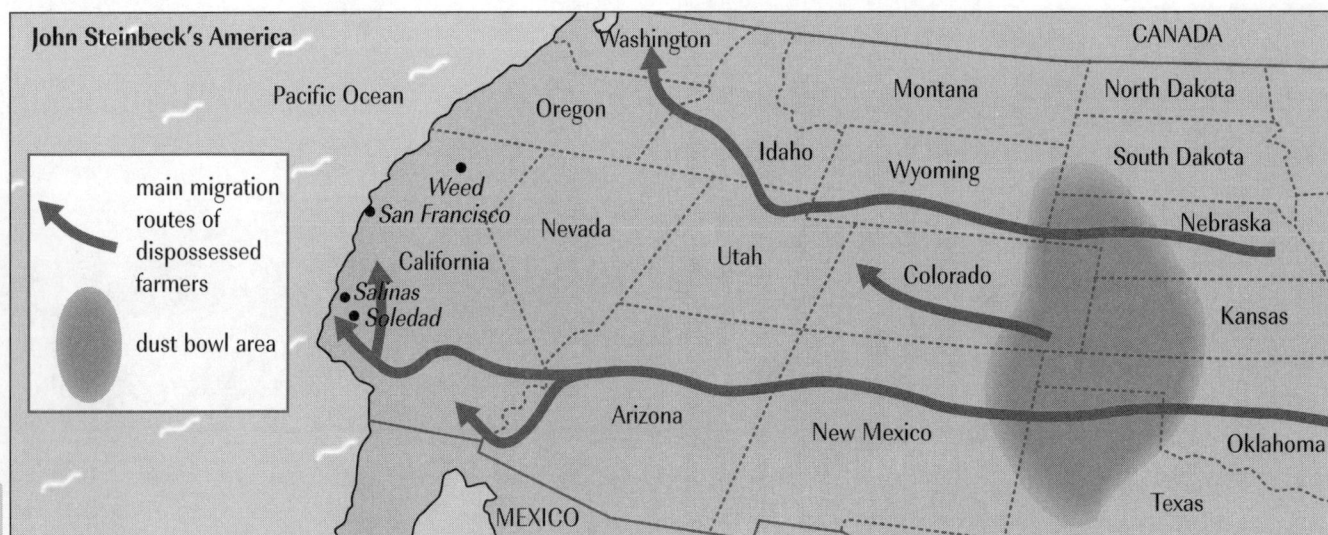

John Steinbeck's America

- main migration routes of dispossessed farmers
- dust bowl area

Pacific Ocean · Washington · CANADA · Oregon · Montana · North Dakota · Idaho · Wyoming · South Dakota · Weed · San Francisco · Nevada · Nebraska · California · Utah · Colorado · Salinas · Soledad · Kansas · Arizona · New Mexico · Oklahoma · MEXICO · Texas

GCSE English & Literature: Exam Preparation Support Pack © HarperCollins *Publishers* 2003

# Of Mice and Men: Plot

→ plot link

----→ thematic or long-term link

George tricks Lennie into jumping into the river

Lennie is grateful to George for rescuing him

George begins to feel responsible for Lennie

Lennie's aunt Clara dies

George and Lennie go on the road together

Curley gets married – it is not a happy relationship

While working in Weed, Lennie tries to stroke a woman's red velvet dress

George and Lennie have to flee Weed

The novel begins . . . . . . . . . . . . . . . . . . . . . . . . . . . . . . . . . . . . . . . . . . .

George and Lennie camp by a stream

George tells Lennie to return to the camp if there is trouble

George and Lennie discuss their dream

George and Lennie arrive at the farm

Curley takes an instant dislike to Lennie

Carlson persuades Candy to let him shoot the dog

Candy overhears George and Lennie discussing their farm

He asks if he can join and promises to add his money to theirs

Slim gives Lennie a puppy

Candy says he wishes he had shot his dog himself

Curley, in search of his wife, has an argument with Slim

Curley tries to take his anger out on Lennie

Lennie crushes his hand

Slim and the others defend Lennie against Curley

Curley hates Lennie

Lennie shares his dream with Crooks

They are interupted by Curley's wife

She takes an interest in Lennie

Lennie is petting his dead puppy when Curley's wife finds him in the barn

She shares her own dreams of escape

Curley's wife allows Lennie to stroke her hair

Lennie accidentally kills her

He flees to the campsite

George finds Lennie

He kills him to protect him from Curley or a lifetime's imprisonment

GCSE English & Literature: Exam Preparation Support Pack © HarperCollins *Publishers* 2003

# Of Mice and Men: Symbols

### George and Lennie's farm

A farm of their own is George and Lennie's ultimate goal. It represents independence from bosses, freedom from fear of the sack and a settled existence for two men who seem to have been on the road for most of their adult lives. Lennie's hope is that it will be a place where he can keep rabbits – but even for George it is a sustaining dream that makes life on the road more bearable. At the beginning of the novel the farm is almost pure fantasy, but Candy's compensation money makes it appear attainable. Candy is taken in almost immediately by George and Lennie's dream. Even the cynical Crooks allows himself a brief dream of moving away from the uncaring ranch. The farm is the book's most powerful symbol, but it is fitting that it is destroyed by Lennie's death. His simple faith in the idea of the farm had been an important element in what kept George going and this is what attracted both Candy and Crooks.

### Curley's wife's film career

At the end of the novel Curley's wife introduces another American dream of escape, Hollywood. Curley's wife felt trapped by her small town existence and dreamed of being a film star. Curley, it seems, married her on the rebound from disappointment in this area but, other than boasting and showing her off as a kind of trophy, Curley seems not to share any of his wife's interests in films. The dream of making it in Hollywood is a common one, and Steinbeck does not seem to value it as much as the life of honest toil imagined by George and Lennie.

### Mice, rabbits and puppies

Several small furry animals meet their deaths at Lennie's hands in the course of the novel. Lennie's interest in them, like his interest in the Weed woman's dress and Curley's wife's hair, is caused by the fact that they are soft and warm. Lennie kills small animals like the puppy because he doesn't know how strong he is and because he tends to panic under emotional stress. (Lennie's inability to deal with stress has two important consequences in the novel, one when he crushes Curley's hand and a second time when he kills Curley's wife.) As with the dream of the farm, Lennie's desire to touch soft and warm things represents an escape from the harsh and cold life of the migrant worker. Lennie's constant failure demonstrates perhaps that there is no escape for men such as him.

### Candy's dog

The episode of Candy's dog foreshadows other aspects of the novel. Candy's dog has outlived its usefulness; its continued existence is unpleasant for the men in the bunkhouse and painful for the dog itself. Candy's attachment to the dog, which he raised from a puppy, is seen as sentimental by the other characters, and even Slim acknowledges that it would be a kindness to put the dog out of its misery. Carlson, on the other hand, does not act out of the dog's best interests; he wants to dispose of the dog because the sight and smell of it upset him. Carlson's selfish action provides a lesson for both Candy and George. Candy regrets that he did not kill the dog himself and sees in its treatment an image of his own future in an uncaring world. George learns from Candy's mistake and realises, when the time comes to put Lennie out of his misery, that he must be the one to do it.

# Of Mice and Men: Themes (1)

### The American Dream

According to the American Dream, anyone can achieve personal success and happiness through hard work. In *Of Mice and Men* almost all the characters dream of a better life. For George and Lennie the good life is symbolised by a farm which will be unaffected by real world economic forces and which will allow them to live off 'the fatta the land'. This dream is eagerly embraced by Candy and is even briefly entertained by the bitter and cynical Crooks. Curley's wife's desire to be a movie star is another version of the same dream; in both cases the fantasy has little connection with reality.

What makes George and Lennie's dream in the novel so powerful is the unexpected chance, provided by Candy, that it might actually come true. The men only have to work solidly for a month to be able to raise the necessary deposit on the farm, but even this is too much to expect in 1930s America. Steinbeck's attitude to the American Dream seems ambivalent. On the one hand it allows people to sustain themselves in harsh and unpleasant circumstances, but on the other it tends to prevent them from acting to change those circumstances.

### Loneliness

A second feature of life for many of the characters in the novel is loneliness. George explains to Lennie early on in the novel that the life of a ranch-hand is profoundly lonely and that the two of them have something that most men in their position lack – companionship. The idea of two men travelling together is so rare that it is treated with suspicion by the Boss and with respect by Slim.

Lennie's childlike innocence prompts Candy, Crooks and Curley's wife to confess their deep sense of isolation. The fact that they admit their fears to an audience as unappreciative as Lennie demonstrates how desperate they are for companionship. Crooks, the only black man in a white community, seems to be the most isolated of all the characters, although Curley's wife, the only woman, runs him a close second.

Life without friendship is terribly empty, and the reader feels profoundly sad for George when he is forced to kill his friend Lennie. Throughout the novel we gain insights into the lonely, dislocated and rootless lives of migrant workers, for instance in the episode concerning the letter. The implication is that loneliness and isolation are a fact of life and that escape is virtually impossible for the labouring poor.

### Male friendship

George and Lennie seem to possess the antidote to loneliness. At the beginning of the novel they are sustained on their travels by their friendship and by their shared dream. When their dream almost becomes a reality it provides a model of male contentment – a place of work and moderate play beyond the reach or bosses, banks and even wives. The loss of this dream is one of the tragic features of the novel.

Crooks points out that the dream is common and that he has seen countless men try and fail to attain it. Nevertheless, he himself is caught up in Lennie and Candy's enthusiasm and cannot resist wondering if there might be a place for him on the farm. The ideal represented by the farm is one of brotherly love in which men come together to care for each other and look after each other's interests. This is in direct contrast to the harsh, exploitative, macho world that represents their daily existence. Unfortunately *Of Mice and Men* demonstrates that such a social organisation is impossible in the real world; either personal, economic or social forces conspire against it.

# Of Mice and Men: Themes (2)

## Women

Women have a very limited place in *Of Mice and Men*. George and Lennie's trouble in Weed was the result of a misunderstanding between Lennie and a woman in a red dress, and Lennie's death is the result of his encounter with Curley's wife. With the exception of Aunt Clara, George is profoundly suspicious of women. Even though he tells Lennie off for his behaviour in Weed, he warns him that women always cause trouble. Except for his sexual needs, which can be satisfied in a brothel, George has no desire for female companionship.

George warns Lennie against women again when they meet Curley's wife at the ranch. She seems to confirm George's suspicions and behaves in a way that is almost calculated to cause trouble. She flirts with Lennie and threatens to use her sexuality to get Crooks into trouble. It is only at the end of the novel that we learn that Curley's wife is as desperate and lonely as the men on the ranch. She is the only woman there and finds that her marriage to Curley, which was meant to be an escape from her small town life, is just as limited and restricting. She wants friendship and companionship just like the men, but the only way she knows to get male attention is through her sexuality. This makes her a disruptive influence on the ranch, as is shown by the dispute between Curley and Slim, and it makes her a danger to the innocent Lennie.

Like the men, Curley's wife has a dream of escape, and so her death means the destruction of all the dreams in the novel. Although she is not as bad as she at first appears, Curley's wife has no place in the world of men and in the idealised vision of brotherly love that the novel presents.

## Oppression and exploitation

*Of Mice and Men* does not offer a simple vision of poor people being oppressed and exploited by the rich, even though the chief villain is the boss's son. Instead the novel explores the way in which poor people are often their own worst enemies. The lonely people on the ranch are forced to take whatever comfort they can by confiding their secrets to strangers, and when that doesn't work they gain satisfaction from attacking others. Curley, because of his height and his sexual insecurity, is constantly on the lookout for trouble, but even Crooks finds a perverse pleasure in forcing Lennie to imagine life without George. Curley's wife admits that her marriage is unhappy but is not above threatening Crooks with a lynching. Helpless characters seem to lash out at those who are weaker and more vulnerable than themselves.

## A tragedy of fate or of character?

*Of Mice and Men* is a tragic novel – but what kind of tragedy does it describe?

### The best laid schemes – a tragedy of fate

The novel takes its title from a Robert Burns poem, 'To a Mouse', which contains the lines:

> *The best laid schemes o' Mice and Men,*
> *Gang aft a-gley [i.e. often go astray].*

The implication for the novel is that George and Lennie are doomed to failure from the start. Their plan for the farm begins as a fantasy and presumably would have ended as a fantasy if they had not met Candy. Unfortunately Curley lived on the same ranch as Candy and the same set of circumstances that brought George and Lennie hope also brought them despair. Crooks's perspective is that all men who entertain dreams of a little piece of land ultimately fail. This view of the novel sees it as a tragedy of fate or bad luck.

### Lennie's bad things – a tragedy of character

The novel begins with George and Lennie on the run from trouble caused by Lennie in Weed. As the story progresses, Lennie crushes Curley's hand and has to be slapped in the face to get him to release Curley. When Crooks invites Lennie to imagine that George has been harmed, Lennie reacts frighteningly. In addition, he kills the puppy and has a history of inadvertently harming other animals. Lennie's fondness for soft things and his tendency to panic in a crisis make him a tragedy waiting to happen. Curley's wife just happens to be the victim. This reading of the novel makes it a tragedy of character.

GCSE English & Literature: Exam Preparation Support Pack © HarperCollins *Publishers* 2003

# Of Mice and Men: Characters (1)

## ◀ Lennie Small

### Actions

Lennie is a huge, immensely strong man with the mind of a child. He likes to pet soft things and this desire is both the focus of his ambitions and the cause of many of his problems. Before the book opens Lennie's attempt to stroke a girl's red velvet dress lead to accusations of rape and a day spent hiding in a ditch avoiding pursuers. Lennie begins the novel stroking a pet mouse, but it is too small to survive his attentions and has to be thrown away for hygienic reasons. In the absence of the mouse, Lennie focuses on the rabbits that he will one day keep on the farm that he and George plan to buy.

Once on the ranch Lennie's great strength means that he secures work easily, but his size arouses the antagonism of the short, sexually insecure Curley. Curley's initial dislike of Lennie becomes hatred when Lennie crushes Curley's hand. Lennie and George's discussion of their plans for their farm is overheard by Candy who says that he can supply money to make the dream farm a reality, but Lennie is just as excited by the gift of a puppy from Slim. His enthusiasm for the puppy takes Lennie to the stable where he meets Crooks, the black stable hand, who disturbs him with the idea that the absent George might not return.

After a further discussion with Candy about the farm, which draws even Crooks in, the three men are disturbed by Curley's wife. She confides her loneliness to the three men but a newly confident Candy rebuffs her. She in turn threatens Crooks but her interest has been aroused in the man who injured her husband. It is when she seeks Lennie out the next day that she is accidentally killed. Lennie returns to the stream where the novel began, and is killed by George to protect him from jail, an asylum or Curley's revenge.

### Role

Lennie's innocent nature means that people are less defensive around him than they usually are; this means that he acts as an unwitting confidant to people such as Candy, Crooks and Curley's wife. Lennie does not seek or particularly appreciate these confidences, but they do enable the reader to gain insights into the characters involved.

Lennie's great size acts as a catalyst for one of the most dramatic moments in the novel. The undersized Curley takes an instant dislike to Lennie and he attempts to engage him in a fight after being faced down by Slim. Lennie's frozen panic demonstrates his inability to cope in a crisis and his crushing of Curley's hand shows his great strength. Precisely the same qualities result in the death of Curley's wife later in the novel. In the immediate aftermath of the fight the men in the bunkhouse act together in a powerful way to protect Lennie against unfair dismissal.

Central to Lennie's role in the novel is his friendship with George. The opening scene gives the reader a clear view of the relationship's strengths and weaknesses. On the one hand Lennie is constantly doing bad things, getting the two of them into trouble and losing them jobs. On the other hand Lennie and George have something that other migrant workers do not have: someone to care about. Lennie essentially calls George's bluff when he threatens to go off into the mountains and George is forced to restate their mutual support. In addition to being travelling companions the two men also share the dream of a farm, which glimmers briefly as a promise to many of the characters in the central section of the novel.

Lennie has relied on George since the death of his Aunt Clara, and there is little doubt that without George Lennie would have been institutionalised, if not imprisoned. However, the relationship is a mutual one, and the George that the reader sees at the end of the novel is a greatly diminished figure.

GCSE English & Literature: Exam Preparation Support Pack © HarperCollins *Publishers* 2003

## George Milton

### Actions

George Milton, a small wiry man, provides the brains to Lennie's brawn. At the beginning of the novel he speaks and acts like an exasperated parent as he warns, cajoles and guides Lennie through their night's camping; he even finishes off with a bedtime story. Lennie's behaviour in Weed had lost them work and involved a brush with the law, so George tells Lennie to return to their campsite if there is further trouble. This conversation sets up the final scene in the story when George kills Lennie out of friendship.

At the ranch George steers Lennie through the process of gaining a job and settling into the bunkhouse. As he does so George tries to warn Lennie of the dangers of the ranch, in particular getting involved with either Curley or his wife. Sadly an encounter with Curley is inevitable and it is George's role to guide Lennie through it. Only when George gives him permission does Lennie fight back against Curley's attack. When Candy learns of the plan for the farm he too gives himself over to George as the prime mover and organiser. Slim seems to like and respect George and to appreciate the friendship between George and Lennie. It is in a conversation with Slim that we learn that George's early relationship with Lennie was characterised by cruelty. George persuaded Lennie to jump into a river when he couldn't swim – Lennie was tremendously grateful when George pulled him out, leaving the latter with a burden of guilt.

It would be unfair to blame George too much, but his absence in town allows Lennie to be singled out by Curley's wife and his participation in the horseshoe game distracts him from Lennie for long enough for the murder to be committed. George has learned through the episode of Candy's dog that if anyone was going to put Lennie out of his misery it had to be him. In killing Lennie he destroys not just a friend but the dream they shared as well.

### Role

The friendship between George and Lennie allows Steinbeck to articulate the dreams and desires of many migrant workers. Their long relationship means that conversations between them have an almost ritualistic quality, and Lennie knows some parts of their talk about the farm off by heart. In the day-to-day world George keeps Lennie out of trouble as much as possible. This is shown by the two men's conversation with the Boss and in the many warnings that George delivers throughout the story.

George's role as organiser and planner is also evident in his relationship with Candy. Candy is prepared to give over his life savings to achieve the dream farm, and at the end of the novel Candy's last hopes are dashed when George decides that the farm project cannot go ahead without Lennie.

George appears to have the upper hand in his friendship with Lennie, but the first night reveals that George is also dependent on Lennie. Admittedly Lennie causes a great deal of trouble, but at least he saves George from the general migrant worker curse of loneliness. When the time comes for George to shoot Lennie the reader understands that he is acting in Lennie's best interests and that George is killing part of himself as well.

GCSE English & Literature: Exam Preparation Support Pack © HarperCollins *Publishers* 2003

## Candy

### Actions

Candy has been crippled by an accident on the ranch and is unusual in that he has permanent employment. Unfortunately Candy can see that his days as a swamper are numbered and that when he can no longer do his job he will be sacked. Candy's dog mirrors his own situation. It too has outlived its usefulness after a full and active life on the ranch and it too is in danger of being 'canned' in a more permanent way than Candy. Only Candy's charity can keep the dog alive and when Carlson insists on shooting it, to put it out of its misery, Candy has no choice but to let the dog go. Only after Carlson has shot the dog does Candy realise that he owed it to the dog to shoot it himself.

Candy's main contribution to the plot of the novel is the compensation money that promises to turn George and Lennie's dream of a farm into reality. It is unlikely that George would ever have been able to earn and keep enough money to buy it on his own. For a brief period it seems that the dream is really attainable; the effect of this change in his circumstances can be seen when the normally self-effacing Candy faces up to Curley's wife in the stable scene. After the death of Lennie, Candy attempts to pursue his dream but as far as George is concerned it is over.

### Role

Candy makes an important contribution to the plot and he is useful as a source of background information for life on the farm. His main role within the novel is symbolic. As a worker almost at the end of his useful life he presents a stark picture of the uncaring nature of the world – there is no one to look out for him and, like his dog, he is at the mercy of stronger men. He also shows how a life of work has made him dependent on his employers – once they cast him off he might as well be dead. He seems unable to make his own decisions, and when he offers George and Lennie his money he seems to be exchanging one type of dependence for another.

As the owner of the dog Candy teaches George an important lesson about caring and responsibility. He loves the dog but when the time comes for it to be put down he shirks the task of killing it. This, he quickly realises, is unfair to the dog and a betrayal of their relationship. He confides his regret to George and, later in the novel, George does not make the same mistake.

## Curley

### Actions

Curley is the son of the ranch owner and the chief villain of the novel. He is not very tall and is constantly aggressive in compensation. He has some reputation as a boxer and is generally feared and despised by the men of the ranch. Curley's aggressive tendencies are made worse by his recent marriage. He seems to have no idea of how to interact with his wife other than in the bedroom, and so his days are spent making sure that she does not come into contact with other men.

Curley dislikes Lennie as soon as he sees him because of his size and it is almost inevitable that Curley will pick a fight with Lennie to establish his dominance. The fight occurs as a result of an accusation aimed at Slim, which Slim denies. In the way of bullies Curley picks on Lennie when he sees that Slim will not be intimidated. Curley is doubly humiliated by the crushing of his hand and then by the stand that the men take against him, and it is clear that there will be no peace for Lennie on the ranch thereafter.

After the killing of his wife, Curley organises the manhunt for Lennie and anticipates killing Lennie in a painful manner. It is partly to save Lennie from Curley that George kills him.

### Role

Curley is pretty much a stage villain. He is defined early on as 'mean' and his dislike of tall men makes a conflict with Lennie inevitable. His treatment of his wife as little more than a sex object and a possession increases the reader's sympathy for her. In the final stages of the novel he acts as a rather unpleasant kind of avenger, motivated not by grief at her death but by the opportunity to get back at the man who crushed his hand.

GCSE English & Literature: Exam Preparation Support Pack © HarperCollins *Publishers* 2003

## Curley's wife

### Actions

Early on in the novel Curley's wife seems to live up (or probably down) to George's opinion of women in general. She is a source of trouble who distracts men and leads them astray. It emerges, however, that she is just as lonely and isolated as the men on the ranch. She confesses to Lennie, Candy and Crooks that her marriage is unhappy, and she confides to Lennie that she too has dreams of escape via the movies. When she allows Lennie to stroke her hair she precipitates her own death and the tragic ending of the novel.

### Role

Curley's wife is cast as the *femme fatale* against Lennie's innocent and Curley's villain, but Steinbeck presents her more sympathetically than is strictly necessary for such a role. Her main problem is that the only way she has learned to communicate with men is through flirting. It is not at all clear that she wants to be unfaithful to Curley, but it is clear that she is desperately lonely and bored on the ranch. She will even spend time with 'losers' like Lennie, Crooks and Candy rather than face neglect by Curley. When Candy stands up to her, Curley's wife again uses her sexuality, this time to threaten Crooks with a rape accusation. Her marginal position on the ranch is emphasised by the fact that we never learn her name and she is defined only in terms of her marriage to Curley.

Curley's wife is another of the novel's victims. She was exploited by the man who said he could get her into the movies, she is used by Curley and she is eventually murdered by Lennie. In all these instances all she ever wanted was some human warmth and companionship, but in *Of Mice and Men* even such simple desires are beyond the reach of ordinary people.

## Crooks

### Actions

Crooks is the stable buck at the ranch and appears in only one scene of the novel. He pours scorn on Lennie's relationship with George and he is sceptical about their plans for a farm. In spite of all of this, however, Crooks cannot resist imagining a place for himself on the farm. When Curley's wife appears he retreats back into his usual morose self.

### Role

As the only black man on the ranch and in the neighbourhood Crooks is the most isolated character in the novel. He has retreated into himself and into books in order to maintain his dignity, but his encounter with Lennie shows that he is just as hungry for real human contact as everyone else. Crooks's conversation with Lennie puts the dream of the farm and the two men's friendship into perspective. He has seen countless men with the same dream and none that achieved it. In probing George's loyalty Crooks almost unleashes Lennie's anger, showing how close to the surface it is in any moment of crisis.

## Slim

### Actions

Slim is the jerkline skinner at the ranch; as a skilled, experienced worker he is valued and appreciated by the other men. Even Curley is reluctant to face up to Slim when he wrongly accuses him of meeting up with his wife. Slim is a quiet man who has a natural air of authority. It is his support of Carlson that convinces Candy that his dog must be shot, and it is to Slim that George confides the story of his early dealings with Lennie. He is generous in his respect for George and Lennie's friendship and he understands why George killed Lennie at the end. Slim's gift of a puppy to Lennie leads to Lennie's presence in the barn where he meets Crooks and where he finally kills Curley's wife.

### Role

Slim is one of the most sympathetic characters in the novel. He listens with understanding to others and he uses the power that he gains and the respect that others pay to him wisely. We glimpse how powerful he could be when he stands up to Curley. If there is a criticism to be made of Slim, it is that he does not act for the good of others often enough.

GCSE English & Literature: Exam Preparation Support Pack © HarperCollins *Publishers* 2003

### Narrative technique

Steinbeck's letters reveal that he planned the book as a combination of novel and play, and it would be very easy to recast the book as a play script. Each section begins with a description of a place – the stream, the bunkhouse, Crooks's room, the stable and the stream – and continues in that place until the action is over. The action is described sparingly, as in a stage direction, and the dialogue provides the reader with most of the story.

At the heart of the novel is its dialogue. This is very naturalistic: people use curses, slang and dialect throughout. Here is George in the opening section:

> 'Jes' a little stretch down the highway,' he says. 'Jes' a little stretch. God damn near four miles, that's what it was! Didn't wanta stop at the ranch gate, that's what. Too God damn lazy to pull up. Wonder he isn't too damn good to stop in Soledad at all. Kicks us out and says: 'Jes' a little stretch down the road.' I bet it was more than four miles. Damn hot day.'

The voices of the characters are not clearly delineated in the novel, although we might notice George's tendency to curse and Lennie's childlike tendency to insert George's name into many of his statements:

> 'I forgot,' Lennie said softly. 'I tried not to forget. Honest to God I did, George.'

In the descriptive passages Steinbeck is inclined to be more poetic. Here is part of his description of the scene after Curley's wife's death:

> As happens sometimes, a moment settled and hovered and remained for much more than a moment. And sound stopped and movement stopped for much, much more than a moment.

The repetition and alliteration in these sentences give them a calm and peaceful air as silence falls over the body of the dead woman. The repeated 'and's achieve a rhythm that is similar to the prayers heard at the end of a church service.

### Point of view

*Of Mice and Men* uses a third-person narrator centred on either George or Lennie. All of the scenes in the book feature one or other of these characters, apart from the brief scene-setting sections such as the introduction and the descriptions of the bunkhouse, Crooks's room and the stable. As an all-knowing narrator Steinbeck is free to report on the thoughts and feelings of the characters, but in general he allows the reader to understand them through action and dialogue.

### Narrative structure and foreshadowing

The story takes place over a period of slightly less than two days and moves forward continuously, although we do learn some background information from the dialogue. In terms of place, the story begins and ends at the stream where George and Lennie camp.

Steinbeck adds to this simple structure by using a technique called foreshadowing. This means that the events early in the book look forward to later ones. A minor example of this is the events in Weed that foreshadow the episode with Curley's wife. The most obvious example concerns the killing of Candy's dog. Candy's dog and Lennie are shot with the same gun for similar reasons, and Candy's bitter remark that he should have killed his dog himself enables the reader to understand why George shoots Lennie.

# A Kestrel for a Knave: Setting and background

## About the author

Barry Hines was born near Barnsley, Yorkshire, in 1939. A miner's son, he was educated at Ecclesfield Grammar School and worked as an apprentice mining surveyor, a labourer and a blacksmith's assistant before training to become a PE teacher. He also played professional football for Barnsley FC. His first novel, *The Blinder*, was published in 1966 and *A Kestrel for a Knave* followed in 1968. *Kes*, a film of the novel, directed by Ken Loach, was released in 1974.

## Setting

**The estate.** *A Kestrel for a Knave* is set on a council estate on the edge of an unnamed northern city. The principal industry seems to be coal mining. The estate itself seems rundown and neglected; fences have been knocked down and not replaced; trees are protected by 'cylinders of close fitting spikes' but the trees inside are dead; and a parade of identically designed shops promises little excitement for the consumer. Billy says that the main form of entertainment available on the estate is 'roamin' t'streets doin' nowt''. Those who live on the estate are regarded with suspicion by outsiders. Mr Porter, Billy's employer, says 'they're all alike off that estate. They'll take your breath if you're not careful.'

Billy's house seems to be more neglected than most. There are no curtains on the windows and no carpets on the floor. Billy shares a bed with his half-brother, Jud, and there seems to be very little furniture elsewhere in the house. Heat is provided by an open fireplace, and if Billy wants to get warm he has to make the fire himself.

**Firs Hill.** Billy delivers papers in an altogether more prosperous community where the houses are set back from the road and separated by tall trees and hedges. The houses Billy sees on his paper round have carpets, central heating and, more importantly for Billy, they appear to contain happy, well-ordered and caring families.

**The school.** At the centre of Billy's daily life is the school, but with the exception of Mr Farthing, it is as bleak and uncaring an environment as the estate. Discipline is harsh and often arbitrary, the teachers as well as the students engage in bullying and the careers officer seems to have fewer ideas about careers than Billy himself.

**The pit.** This is where Jud works and where Billy knows he doesn't want to go. It seems to be the only major employer in the area but the work is hard, monotonous and exhausting. If Jud's bet had been placed he would have used his winnings to take a week off work.

**The farm.** The estate is on the edge of the city and there is easy access to the countryside. The farm is where Billy finds relief from the bleak life of the estate and, of course, where he finds Kes.

GCSE English & Literature: Exam Preparation Support Pack © HarperCollins *Publishers* 2003

# A Kestrel for a Knave: Plot

| Time | Event |
|---|---|
| 6.00 a.m. | The alarm wakes Billy and Jud. Jud punches Billy, deliberately pulls off the warm blankets and takes Billy's bike. |
| 7.00 a.m. | Billy has to make the fire. There is no milk.<br>Billy has to run to the newsagent's as Jud has taken his bike. He steals chocolate.<br>He walks his newspaper round through the well-off suburb.<br>He steals orange juice and eggs from a milk float.<br>He reads 'Desperate Dan' in *The Dandy* comic.<br>He returns home and argues with his mother about getting things on credit from the shop.<br>There is no tea in the house and Billy has no breakfast.<br>Billy goes to see his kestrel. |
| flashback | Billy remembers going to collect the kestrel from its nest. |
| 9.00 a.m. | School<br>**Registration.** Billy makes a joke about the shipping forecast.<br>**Assembly.** Billy, thinking of his kestrel, does not sit down on cue. He is told to go to the head's office for punishment.<br>**Head's office.** Billy is caned along with some smokers and an innocent messenger.<br>**English lesson.** The class is studying fact and fiction with Mr Farthing.<br>The story of the tadpoles.<br>Billy tells about training his kestrel – Mr Farthing is fascinated.<br>Billy writes a 'Tall Story' about his father. |
| 10.30 a.m. | **Break.** Fight with MacDowall. Mr Farthing intervenes and chats with Billy.<br>**PE lesson.** Billy has no kit and is made to wear huge shorts by Mr Sugden.<br>He is chosen last for his team and put in goal.<br>Billy helps to remove a dog from the field.<br>Mr Sugden traps Billy in the freezing showers for letting in a goal. |
| 12.30 p.m. | **Lunch time.** Billy misses school lunch to go home to feed Kes.<br>Mr Farthing arrives and watches as Billy flies her in the field.<br>Jud has left instructions for a complicated 5/- bet.<br>Billy goes to the betting shop and is told that the bet has a very low chance of success.<br>He spends Jud's 5/- on fish, chips and cigarettes. He is also given meat for Kes. |
| 2.00 p.m. | **Maths lesson.** Billy sees Jud looking for him. He realises something is wrong and hides in the boiler room.<br>**Careers interview.** Billy doesn't want to work in a mine, but there are few other choices. |
| 4.00 p.m. | Billy runs all the way home to find the hut broken into and no kestrel inside. He searches desperately.<br>At the betting shop Billy learns that Jud's horses came in and that he would have won a great deal of money.<br>Billy searches everywhere but without success. |
| 6.00 p.m. | Billy returns home to find Jud and his mother.<br>There is a violent argument, as Jud would have won a week's wages.<br>Jud could not find Billy at school so he killed Kes instead.<br>Billy finds Kes's body in the bin and attacks Jud.<br>His mother can't understand the fuss about 'only a bird'.<br>Billy runs out of the house. |
| 7.00 p.m. until late | On the City Road Billy remembers a time when he went to the cinema with his dad.<br>On their return home there was another man in the house and his dad left after an argument.<br>Billy fantasises about revenge.<br>He goes home to an empty house. |

GCSE English & Literature: Exam Preparation Support Pack © HarperCollins *Publishers* 2003

# A Kestrel for a Knave: Symbols and themes (1)

## Kes

The principal symbol in *A Kestrel for a Knave* is the kestrel. Its first application can be seen in the title, which comes from the piece of verse about falconry quoted at the front of some editions of the novel. A fuller version of this ranking of birds is:

> to royalty the gyrfalcon, to an earl the peregrine, to a yeoman the goshawk,
> to a priest the sparrow-hawk, and to a knave or servant the useless kestrel.

The kestrel is at the bottom of the falconry ranking, just as Billy is at the bottom of almost everybody's list of priorities in the novel.

Within the novel the kestrel reflects a number of aspects of Billy's life. He has kept many animals in the past but the kestrel is special because of its strength, independence and beauty. In order to train it to achieve its full potential Billy has to learn to understand the bird's moods, needs and preferences and devote a great deal of time to carefully prepared practices and drills. This is precisely what Billy doesn't have in his own life and education, and with the possible exception of Mr Farthing, the barely literate Billy turns out to be the best educator in the novel.

Even though it is trained, the kestrel is still free when it flies. It is held in place by the love and attention that Billy has lavished on it, and by the rewards it gets for flying well. Compared with this relationship Billy's home life is deeply flawed. Neither Jud nor Billy's mum understand or appreciate Billy's achievement in training the kestrel, and at home he is treated with hostility or indifference. Billy is only free because he is neglected, and he only returns to the house because he has nowhere else to go. Without a great deal of competition Billy, it seems, is the novel's best parent.

Kes also represents a wider world than the one that Billy normally has access to. It represents, in its beauty and strength, a world far removed from the mean streets of the estate and the brutally enforced discipline of the school. It is a bird of prey and it is confident in its power; it does not have to shore up its ego by bullying or belittling those around it; it simply dominates the sky when it is in flight.

When Billy goes to collect the kestrel he leaves the city behind and comes into contact with nature. The descriptions in this section of the book emphasise, in poetic language, the richness of the woodland and hold out a promise of something beyond the ordinary. Training Kes brings some of this back into Billy's life. As he says, Kes is not a tame bird, and contact with his wildness is the closest Billy gets to a spiritual life.

GCSE English & Literature: Exam Preparation Support Pack © HarperCollins *Publishers* 2003

# A Kestrel for a Knave: Symbols and themes (2)

### The family

The word 'dysfunctional' was not in common use in 1968, but Billy's family clearly falls under this definition. The opening sequence of the novel reveals a family characterised by minor cruelties, poor organisation, indifference to the feeling of other family members and a complete lack of nurturing behaviour on the part of Billy's mother. Billy simply has to fend for himself in terms of such basic necessities as food, clothing and warmth. Rather than being supported by his mother and Jud, he is exploited by them, constantly being forced to carry out basic tasks and run errands. As Billy says to Kes, 'Do this, do that, I've got to do everything in this house ...'.

On the day Billy finds Kes we get another glimpse into Casper family life. Jud is contemptuous of Billy's interest in falconry and pours scorn on his attempts to read the book that Billy was forced to steal from the library. Significantly he does not disapprove of Billy stealing, merely of him stealing something as useless as a book:

> Tha must be crackers. ... Nicking books ... I could understand it if it wa' money, but chuff me, not a book ... An' what better off will tha be when tha's read it?

Neither Jud nor Billy's mum really listen to Billy's enthusiasms as they are both too concerned with their own plans for the day. When Jud returns drunk from his night out, Billy is so angered by his loutish and inconsiderate behaviour that he lashes out and beats him. But Jud is too drunk even to chase him.

Violence, the threat of violence and selfish behaviour are constant parts of Billy's home life. When he wakes up, Jud strips the bedclothes from the bed, refuses to re-set the alarm and leaves the light on, all in petty spite because he has to go to work. Billy's mother is too concerned about getting to work herself to bother about feeding Billy – there is no food in the house – and when he answers her back and leaves the house she shouts after him, 'I'll bloody murder you.' In his 'Tall Story' Billy's idea of an impossibly happy day is waking up in a warm house with plenty to eat and drink.

When Jud learns that his bet has not been placed, Billy is in no doubt that Jud would cause him serious harm if he were to find him. As it happens, Billy escapes serious physical harm because Jud seems to feel guilty about killing Kes. The undersized Billy is unable to cause Jud any serious harm either. The real damage is emotional: the worst moment is probably when Billy turns to his mother for comfort and is shrugged off.

Billy's father makes an appearance in his 'Tall Story' and at the end of the novel. As well as the misery of his day-to-day existence, the lack of a father figure in Billy's life clearly troubles him. The strong and silent Kes at least provides someone Billy can talk to and share his troubles with.

### Poverty and social deprivation

An important aspect of the novel is its investigation of poverty and social deprivation. Billy's family should not, in fact, be very poor as Jud would be earning a good wage in the pit and Billy's mum also seems to be employed. The reason for Billy's apparent poverty is lack of care rather than lack of cash. Jud and Billy's mum clearly spends a good deal of their money on entertainment, but neither of them seems to put much effort into providing home comforts for Billy.

It would be simple to accuse Jud and Billy's mum of selfishness, but their desire for some fun in the evening is a response to long days spent in boring, repetitive and, in Jud's case, physically demanding jobs. Because they have to work so much of the time they have little time for home care or for looking after Billy. Education has done little for Jud or Billy's mum, and it seems that it is about to fail Billy as well.

GCSE English & Literature: Exam Preparation Support Pack © HarperCollins *Publishers* 2003

# A Kestrel for a Knave: Symbols and themes (3)

## ◀ Education

The novel's portrait of school life reveals a deeply disturbing picture of neglect, indifference and casual violence. Billy's reading abilities make *The Dandy* a challenge, while his writing is poorly structured and badly spelt. No one at the school seems disturbed that a fifteen-year-old boy has made so little progress in his education, and most of the teachers don't seem to see anything in Billy other than a troublemaker. Yet in looking after Kes Billy has read, understood and applied the content of a complicated book on falconry and shown a great deal of patience, responsibility and care towards another creature.

In 1968, when the novel was written, students were allowed to leave school at fifteen. Since Billy has no interest in exams he would be expected to leave school without any qualifications. Clearly Billy has made little progress after ten years of schooling, but this is not surprising when we see what his daily experience of school is like. Most of the teachers seem to regard Billy and his fellow students in 4C with indifference or as potential problems that need to be controlled. The school environment is dull and boring at best and vandalised at worst.

Billy's school day starts with the aptly named Mr Crossley, who responds with sarcasm to Billy's attempt at humour and continues with an assembly that is a mere formality. Mr Gryce does not even notice when the boy reading the lesson leaves the word 'not' out of 'it is your heavenly Father's will that one of these little ones should be lost', implying that Mr Gryce couldn't care less if one of the little ones in his charge is lost. More shocking than the violence of Mr Gryce's caning session is its routine nature. He appears to be going through the motions of discipline without believing that it will do any good. He is contemptuous of his students and sees them, snobbishly, as spineless 'fodder for the mass media'. At least some of the boys enjoy their PE lesson, but for Billy it is a mixture of humiliation, boredom and bullying. Mr Sugden is hardly a teacher at all, but someone who is working out his personal fantasies at the expense of the students.

The ability of Mr Farthing to engage the boys in a lesson and to encourage Billy to talk and write shows that the students in 4C are not the useless troublemakers that they are assumed to be. He is interested in what the boys have to say, he speaks to them with respect and he insists that the members of the class respect each other. Instead of enlisting the other boys as supporters in his bullying he comes down hard on MacDowall when he breaks up his fight with Billy, and although he is perhaps too aggressive, he at least tempers his violence with a sense of fairness.

The Youth Employment Officer is supposed to be the bridge between the school and the world of work, but he is as lazy and incompetent as the majority of the teachers. He takes no time or trouble to find out about Billy's interests or talents, and he writes him off as a piece of factory fodder.

# A Kestrel for a Knave: Symbols and themes (4)

## Nature

On the day of the novel Billy is mostly trapped within the confines of the ugly estate and his dull school, but in the descriptions of Billy in the fields and woods on his paper round or in his flashbacks concerning Kes he walks in a different and more beautiful world. It is clear that Billy takes great delight in being in the country. This is powerfully conveyed in Barry Hines's descriptions, for instance when Billy observes a dew drop on a blade of grass that:

> had almost forced the blade of grass to the earth, and it lay in the curve of the blade like the tiny egg of a mythical bird. Billy moved his head from side to side to make it sparkle ...

As well as his silent and uncommunicated love of nature, Billy has had a long history of caring for animals such as magpies, jackdaws and even a fox cub. During the games lesson Billy is able to deal with the dog that has wandered onto the football pitch with little trouble; it is clear that he has a special empathy with animals.

## Kes

The creature that means most to Billy is Kes. It is not tame like a conventional pet and it brings something of the wildness and freedom of nature into Billy's daily life. He has spent a great deal of time, energy and patience training it, and it has rewarded Billy's efforts with its loyalty. Billy confides his problems to the bird and he shares its sense of power and freedom when it is in flight.

Mr Farthing discovers a great deal about Billy's love for animals in his lesson and identifies a talent in Billy that might well have formed the basis of a future career. The Youth Employment Officer sees nothing of this in Billy; once he has offered the meagre possibilities of office work, manual work or exams he feels that he has done his job.

When Jud kills Kes an important part of Billy's life is destroyed. When he begins to fear for the bird he runs towards the woods to look for it, but after he has found Kes dead he turns towards the city and the old cinema for comfort.

## Nature – metaphor or Romantic parable?

Barry Hines's use of nature can be seen in two ways, either as a metaphor for any hidden talent or as a Romantic parable. In the first view, Billy's love of animals can be seen simply as something that takes him beyond his normal world and his normal self. Kes is a beautiful and powerful symbol but Billy could equally have been obsessed by cars or working with wood. The point is that people who appear to have nothing special about them often have hidden depths. Billy's desire to care for animals might be a compensation for the lack of care he receives from his family, but it gives him a talent which would, if properly encouraged, make him a valued member of the community. In Billy's school only Mr Farthing is even aware that this might be true.

The second view is that there is something about contact with nature itself that allows human sympathy and compassion to grow. This idea was developed by the French Romantic philosopher Jean-Jacques Rousseau; it was also at the centre of the work of such poets as William Wordsworth. Characters like Billy's mum and Jud operate in a self-centred and brutal world because that is all that the estate and the pit provide them with. Billy has been fortunate to be touched by nature and this has given him a keener appreciation of love and responsibility than the older members of his family. This view of a *A Kestrel for a Knave* places town and country in opposition to each other and demonstrates the fragility of the lessons Billy has learned. Industrial, town-based society has no place for someone like Billy.

GCSE English & Literature: Exam Preparation Support Pack © HarperCollins *Publishers* 2003

# A Kestrel for a Knave: Characters (1)

## ◀ Billy Casper

### Actions

Fifteen-year-old Billy Casper is the centre of the novel which tells of a single day in his life (see Revision Sheet 56). We also learn a number of important facts through flashbacks, memories and conversations. These include: his father has left home as a result of his mother having an affair; Billy has been in trouble with the police; he has been a reformed character since he found and started to train his kestrel, Kes.

The structure of Billy's day consists of a series of ups and downs. For instance, setbacks such as having to walk his paper round are compensated by an opportunity to steal from the milk-float; his fight with MacDowall is followed by a conversation with the one sympathetic adult in the novel, Mr Farthing. The biggest 'up' in Billy's day is his decision not to place Jud's bet. Instead, he is able to buy cigarettes and when he goes to the fish and chip shop he is given an extra portion.

Unfortunately, and literally against all the odds, Jud's gamble is successful. Although Billy avoids Jud in school, this leads to the worst possible 'down' for Billy, the killing of Kes.

### Role

Billy does not at first sight appear to be a very sympathetic character. He lies, cheats and steals, he is rude to his mother and he gets into fights at school. However, this external view of Billy is counteracted by what the reader finds out about him. At home he is bullied by a thuggish half-brother; his mother is too wrapped up in her own concerns to support, or at times even notice, Billy; and Billy's father is absent because of his mother's infidelities. He does not do well at school, but this is not surprising considering the attitude of his teachers towards him and his fellow students; he is bullied by MacDowall because he is trying to break away from former bad influences. Even his stealing of the book on falconry is partially justified by the fact that there was no possibility of getting his mother to sign the necessary forms.

Billy's relationship with Kes is central to his 'reformation' as a character. Because of the bird he has started to avoid troublemaking friends, he has established relationships within the local community and he has accepted the discipline necessary to care for a demanding, but rewarding, pet. All of this is set against the background of a harsh home environment and a complete lack of encouragement from anywhere else. On the day the story takes place the intervention of Mr Farthing seems to promise slightly more hope for the future, but these hopes are dashed by the killing of Kes.

Billy is a victim in almost every aspect of his life, and it is only the existence of Kes that gives him any real joy or excitement. When Kes is killed Billy turns to his mother for emotional support, but all she can manage when he tries to hug her is an embarrassed 'gi' over, Billy.' The novel ends with Billy going to the old cinema and remembering his dad. This suggests that the turning point in Billy's life was that first loss. With the loss of Kes Billy's future looks very bleak indeed.

Billy's story suggests that there is hope for people in deprived homes or in dysfunctional families if they can find a way out through nature, art or any avenue that gives purpose to their existence. The story also illustrates how fragile that hope is.

GCSE English & Literature: Exam Preparation Support Pack © HarperCollins *Publishers* 2003

# A Kestrel for a Knave: Characters (2)

## Billy – hero or anti-hero?

The character of Billy is deeply ambiguous. On the one hand he is the central character of the novel, who gains our sympathy and respect as we read of his achievements, and on the other he is a thief, a liar and a cheat.

If we look at the things that Billy does wrong, like stealing, shaking Mr Porter's ladder, fighting with MacDowall or beating Jud when he was drunk, we can see that more often than not he is provoked. His theft from the milk-float is prompted by hunger and thirst, and his shaking of the ladder follows Mr Porter's ungenerous response to his finishing the paper round on time. His violent bouts with MacDowall and Jud are also provoked by teasing or sheer lack of consideration, and his attack on Jud at the end represents his outraged reaction to the loss of the most precious thing in his life.

It is also possible to see Billy's violence and lack of morality as products of his environment. The teachers at school regularly use violence, such as random slapping of students' heads and caning to keep control, and they are not above enlisting the support of students to join in with their bullying and sarcasm. Billy's former school friends resent the fact that his interest in Kes has taken him away from the kind of behaviour that got him in trouble with the police. At home Jud expresses no disapproval of Billy's stealing, only of the 'useless' thing he stole, a book. Billy's mum neglects him and makes no secret of her casual affairs with men. When she fails to punish Jud it is clear that it is because he is bigger and stronger than her. In such circumstances it is unsurprising that Billy behaves as he does.

The list of things that Billy does right in the novel is, under the circumstances, rather impressive. He holds down a job as newspaper delivery boy in spite of the suspicion and lack of encouragement of his employer; he demonstrates patience and persistence in the extremely difficult task of training a kestrel; he carries out research (even if this does involve stealing the library book); he acts responsibly towards the bird that he has adopted; he shows courage when he climbs the monastery wall to get the bird; he is sensitive to beauty in his environment and responds positively to such things as the sounds of the shipping forecast;

he informs and entertains his class with his account of training Kes; and he refuses to be intimidated by the much bigger and stronger MacDowall.

The simple message that Billy's behaviour in the novel conveys is that people who do bad things are not necessarily bad people.

## Jud

### Actions

Jud is the cause of much of the pain in Billy's life. In the opening passage he meanly takes away Billy's warm blankets and then goes to work on Billy's bike so that Billy has to walk his paper round. At lunchtime he imposes the task of placing a bet on Billy with no concern for Billy's time or other commitments. When the bet succeeds Jud has no compunction about coming to school to exact his revenge on Billy and, of course, it is Jud who eventually kills Kes. In a flashback we see Jud's drunkenness and mockery on the day Billy first found Kes. Even the fight with MacDowall is the result of accusations about Jud being a bastard.

### Role

Jud's role is clearly that of villain. He has almost no redeeming characteristics, and his dealings with Billy on the day the story takes place are the cause of all his unhappiness. However, Barry Hines does provide enough information for the reader not to condemn him out of hand. Jud works as a miner but with little enthusiasm or hope for the future. He values the money he would have made on the bet because he would have been able to take a week off work. It is also clear that Jud has been through the same education system as Billy and has had as little help as Billy to look beyond the confines of life on the estate and work down the pit. Jud is as inclined to bully his mother as much as his brother, but at least he takes his responsibilities as the wage earner seriously. Jud is not a pleasant character but he is the product of an unpleasant system.

In terms of the story, Jud's conflicts with Billy provide moments of high drama. The placing of the bet is central to the development of the plot.

GCSE English & Literature: Exam Preparation Support Pack © HarperCollins *Publishers* 2003

## Billy's mum

### Actions

Billy's mum is shown to be lacking as a mother on every occasion she appears. In the morning of the day described by the book she fights with Billy because he will not go to the shop to buy cigarettes for her. Billy's father is absent because she had an affair, and it is clear that her casual affairs are continuing. In a flashback we see her lack of sympathy and support over getting the kestrel, and when Jud has killed Kes she seems unable to comfort, or even understand, Billy.

### Role

Like Jud, Billy's mum is a negative force in Billy's life. She seems selfish and uncaring and she does not appear to have given Billy very much time or attention. We might sympathise with her as a single parent with a bullying and overbearing older child and a younger child who has been in trouble with the police, but her neglect of her family at even the most basic level can have few excuses.

Billy's mum's appalling character can only increase the reader's sympathy for Billy. We learn through Billy's 'Tall Story', and through other observations that Billy makes, how important family life is to him and how strongly he was affected by the departure of his father. Billy's mum helps the reader to understand how his behaviour is influenced by the people around him, and to see the pain that lies beyond Billy's bland exterior.

## Mr Farthing

### Actions

Billy's English teacher is the only person in the book who takes an interest in Billy. Mr Farthing runs a class that is disciplined, respectful of others and above all interesting. He listens to what his students have to say and addresses them in a friendly conversational manner. He is so fascinated by Billy's account of his kestrel that he takes time out to watch the bird fly. After the lesson Mr Farthing breaks up a fight between Billy and MacDowall and, after savagely telling off MacDowall, he speaks sympathetically to Billy. At lunch time Mr Farthing is deeply impressed by watching Kes fly and there seems some hope that Billy will have at least one sympathetic adult in his life in future.

### Role

Mr Farthing's role in the novel is to suggest that education can reach boys like Billy. Gryce, Crossley, Sugden and the Youth Employment Officer all seem to have given up on their charges and retreated into mindless discipline (Gryce), sarcasm (Crossley), fantasy (Sugden) or indifference (Youth Employment Officer). Even Billy admits that Mr Farthing tries 'to learn us summat". In Mr Farthing's presence Billy is able to talk freely and, through his obvious expertise about the kestrel, gain some respect from his fellow students.

## Mr Gryce

### Actions

Billy's headmaster is a sort of monster of discipline. He punishes students, even innocent messengers, while at the same time appearing to believe that the punishment won't do any good. His morning assembly invokes the Christian message of caring, but he is as deaf to this as to the pleas of the boy who has only come to deliver a message and gets caned instead.

### Role

Gryce demonstrates the casual violence that was a feature of schools before the banning of corporal punishment.

## Mr Sugden

### Actions

Mr Sugden is Billy's PE teacher and the source of yet more pain in Billy's life. He humiliates Billy by forcing him to wear extra large shorts, and he allows the other boys to join him in making fun of Billy. He is biased when he picks the best players for his team, and he unfairly blames Billy for letting in a goal. Like many bullies his bravery only goes so far, and he is more than happy to let Billy deal with the dog wandering onto the pitch – after he has said to Billy, 'What's the matter ... are you scared of the ball?' His final unpleasant act is to keep Billy trapped in the showers as a punishment for letting in the goal.

### Role

Mr Sugden's dreams of grandeur about being a footballer provide a certain amount of comic relief, but they should not blind us to the fact that he is someone who is using the teaching profession for his personal satisfaction. The lesson that he teaches the students is that you can get what you want through bullying and intimidation.

## Mr Crossley

### Actions

Mr Crossley takes the register when Billy arrives in school. He is concerned only with completing his administrative task and shows no rapport with, or understanding of, the students. He doesn't get Billy's comment about 'German Bight' coming after 'Fisher' in the weather forecast and he responds to Billy with sarcasm.

### Role

Mr Crossley is similar to Gryce but uses verbal rather than physical violence to control the students.

## Youth Employment Officer

### Actions

The Youth Employment Officer interviews Billy for careers advice, and completely fails to give him any. He doesn't understand Billy and seems to have very little interest in finding out about him. He gives Billy a leaflet and suggests that, as he isn't interested in taking exams, he will probably end up down the pit.

### Role

The Youth Employment Officer extends the story of Billy's life into the future. He demonstrates how an uncaring and ignorant education system seems designed to not to cope with the needs and talents of boys like Billy.

## MacDowall

### Actions

MacDowall's most significant action in the story was not to do something. He was supposed to go bird's nesting with Billy and Tibbut on the day that Billy found Kes, but his mother wouldn't get him out of bed when Billy called. Billy's finding of Kes thus coincided with a break with a 'friend' who had been a bad influence. On the day covered by the novel MacDowall's resentment at being abandoned as a friend spills over into the fight that Mr Farthing breaks up.

### Role

MacDowall is a younger version of Jud and an example of the kind of boy that Billy has been saved from by his relationship with Kes. However, Billy doesn't appear to have any other friends at school and so spending so much time with Kes also represents some kind of sacrifice.

# A Kestrel for a Knave: Language and style

## The authorial voice

The novel uses centred third person narration. This means that the reader is only told about what happens to Billy, and only Billy's thoughts and feelings are reported on. This method of telling the story has many of the advantages of a first-person narration without the disadvantages of being confined to the kinds of things a barely literate boy might be expected to write. (See 'A Tall Story' for an example of the way Billy himself writes.)

The narration is generally a record of what happens to Billy, and there are no explicit comments on events. However, the narrative voice is at times distinctly poetic. This is particularly noticeable in the descriptions of the countryside.

## Other voices

A great deal of the feel of the novel is created by dialogue. The character's accents are shown through the spelling and a number of Yorkshire dialect terms are used. The most noticeable Yorkshire features are the use of 'thi' and 'tha' for standard English 'you', and the shortening of 'the' to 't''. Billy and his family use this kind of language consistently, often shortening familiar words and expressions, and on many occasions peppering their speech with threats of violence and insults.

As well as those in Billy's family there are several other voices in the novel. Mr Farthing and Mr Gryce represent educated adults, although Mr Gryce seems to communicate in clichés and other unthinking expressions that suggest that he has stopped thinking about the world around him. Mr Farthing uses more formal speech than the boys but he is not superior about this. In talking to the class, or Billy, he uses shortened forms and question tags to encourage further communication:

> 'Just think, you'll be leaving school in a few weeks, starting your first job, meeting fresh people. That's something to look forward to isn't it?'

Another extended voice that we meet is that of Anderson, the boy who bet his friend that he wouldn't dare to put his feet in a wellington boot full of tadpoles. This extended narrative provides a full and light-hearted example of Yorkshire speech.

When Billy commits his thoughts to paper in 'A Tall Story' we see the gap between his ability to talk and write. He has held the class enthralled by his description of how he trained the kestrel, but his writing is lacking in detail and is full of errors. Unfortunately, the world tends to judge people on how well they can write rather than how well they can speak.

## Narrative technique

The story takes place in a single day, from early in the morning until quite late at night. The background to the story, such as the finding of and training of Kes, is presented either in flashbacks or revealed in conversation. The first flashback takes place when Billy is tending the bird in the morning; the second occurs during morning assembly. The main conversations are with Mr Farthing – both during his lesson and when he comes to see Kes fly. A brief flashback, triggered by the death of Kes and the sight of an old cinema, concerns the night Billy's father left home.

This technique highlights the difference between Billy's inner and outer life. His daily life is dull at best and painful and violent at worst. Billy from the outside is purposeless and almost hopeless. From the inside, until the death of Kes Billy's life is vibrant and highly focused.

GCSE English & Literature: Exam Preparation Support Pack © HarperCollins *Publishers* 2003

# To Kill a Mockingbird: Setting and background

## About the author

*To Kill a Mockingbird* is the only published novel of Nelle Harper Lee. She was born in 1926 in Monroeville, in Monroe County, southwest Alabama, at that time a town of about 7,000 people. She is the youngest of four children of Amasa Coleman Lee and Frances Finch Lee. The novel appeared in 1960 and became an instant success. Harper Lee has since received many honours, including the prestigious Pulitzer Prize, but she has always avoided publicity.

Maycomb, the town in which the novel is set, is said to be a thinly veiled portrait of Monroeville. The plan (right) shows the layout of Monroeville in the 1920s, with houses and other locations from *To Kill a Mockingbird* marked. The character of Atticus Finch is widely regarded as a portrait of Harper Lee's father, Amasa. There is also a clear parallel between the trial of Tom Robinson and the Scottsboro, Alabama, rape trials of April 1931. Nine young black men, accused of raping two white women, were nearly lynched before their trial and were not provided with a lawyer until the first day in court. The all-white jury found the men guilty and sentenced all but the youngest, aged twelve, to death. This was in spite of medical evidence that the women had not been raped. The verdict was repealed later and all but one of the men were later freed or paroled. Lee was only five years old at the time of these events.

## Race in America

Alabama is one of the Southern states of America which attempted to leave the United States over the issue of slavery, amongst other things. The Confederate States of America, which Alabama joined, were defeated in the American Civil War (1861–5) and all the slaves were freed. This did not mean, however, that former slaves were treated equally. Although they were free in theory, the Southern states made voting rights conditional on property and education. When 'legal' discrimination did not work, terror was employed by organisations such as the Ku Klux Klan. These masked raiders frequently attacked black people, Catholics and Jews in the 1920s.

Black Americans organised to fight for equal rights. In 1909 the National Association for the Advancement of

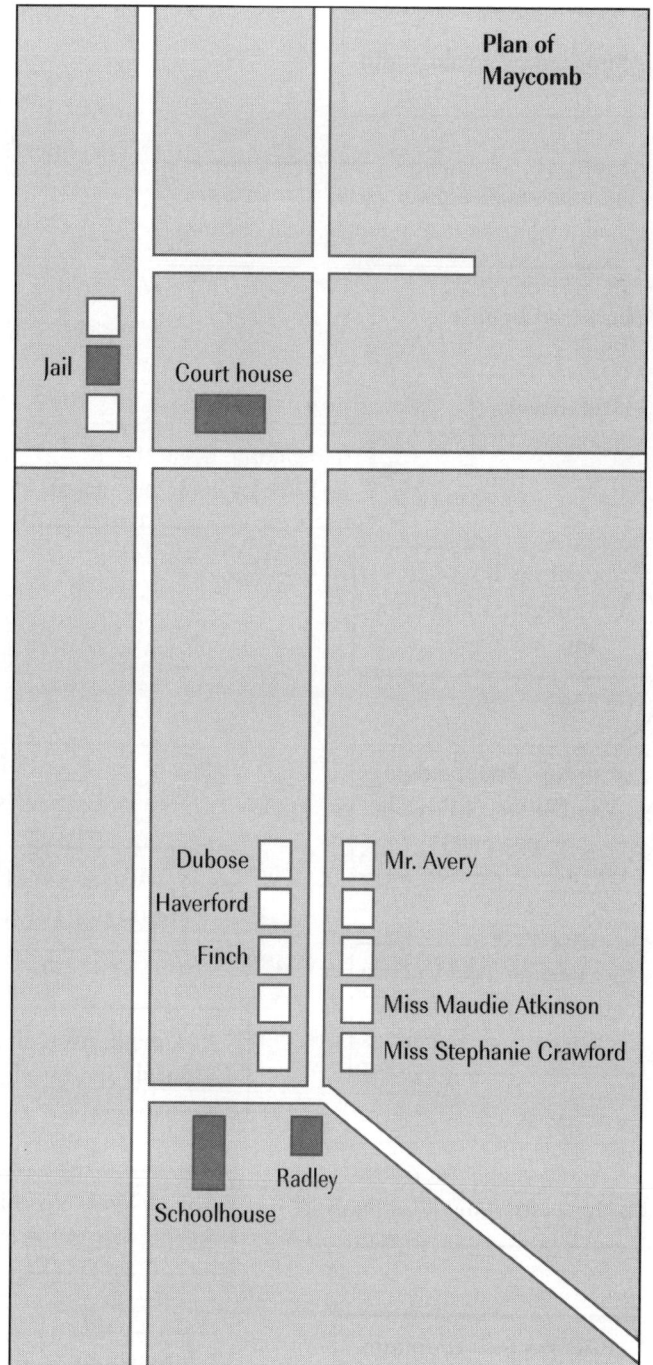

Plan of Maycomb

Colored People (NAACP) was formed. The movement was given a great boost by the fact that black and white troops fought alongside each other during the Second World War, but serious protests did not begin to take place until the 1950s. In 1957 the Rev. Martin Luther King led a successful boycott campaign against segregation on buses. Also in 1957 the United States government called out federal troops to allow nine black children to go to an all-white school in Little Rock, Alabama, where State troops had been used to turn them away. It was in the context of these protests against racism that *To Kill a Mockingbird* was published.

# To Kill a Mockingbird: Plot

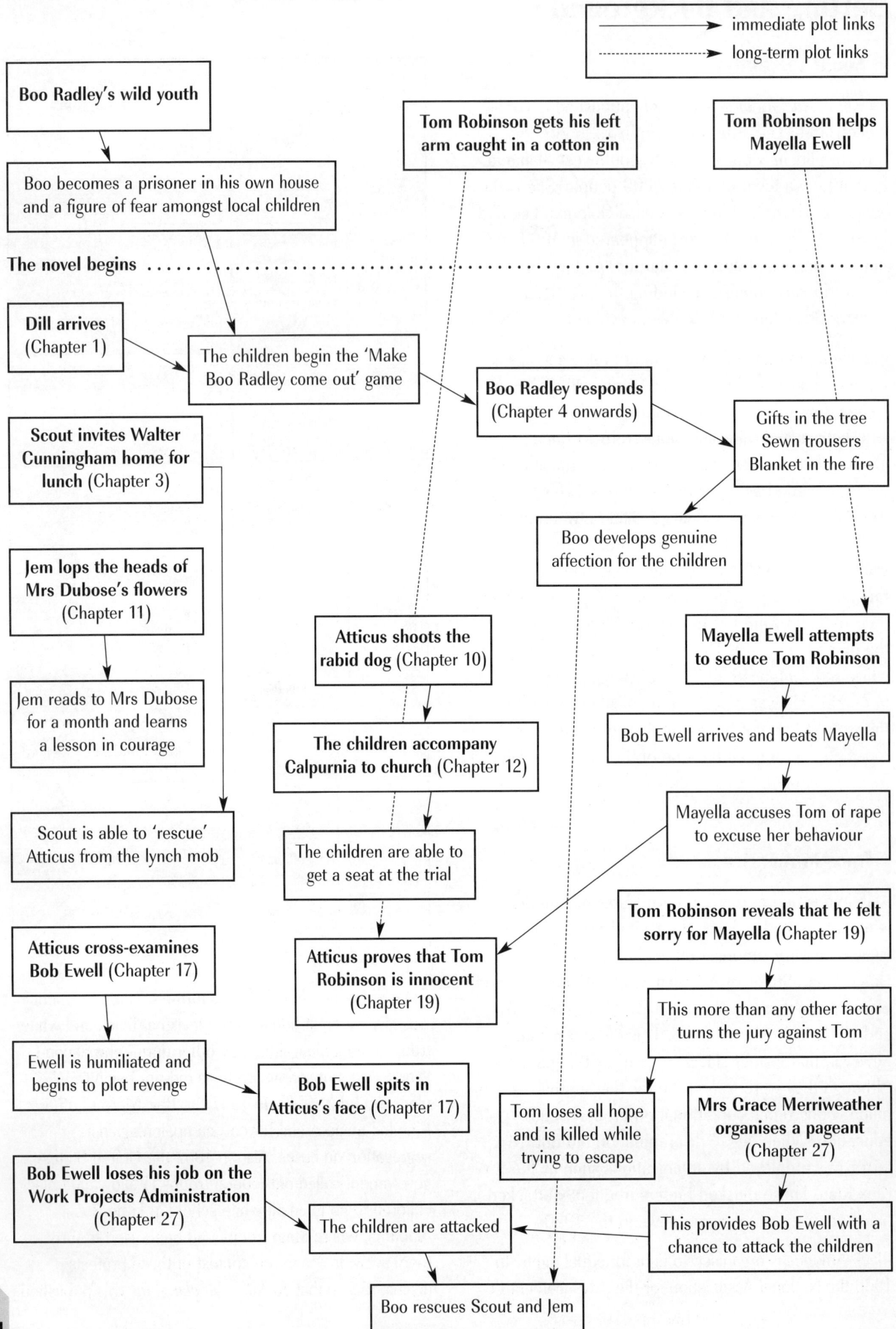

→ immediate plot links

⤍ long-term plot links

**Boo Radley's wild youth**

Boo becomes a prisoner in his own house and a figure of fear amongst local children

**Tom Robinson gets his left arm caught in a cotton gin**

**Tom Robinson helps Mayella Ewell**

**The novel begins** . . . . . . . . . . . . . . . . . . . . . . . . . . . . . . . . . . . . . . . . . . . . . . . . . . . . . . . . . . . . . . . . . . . . . . . . . . .

**Dill arrives** (Chapter 1)

The children begin the 'Make Boo Radley come out' game

**Boo Radley responds** (Chapter 4 onwards)

Gifts in the tree Sewn trousers Blanket in the fire

**Scout invites Walter Cunningham home for lunch** (Chapter 3)

Boo develops genuine affection for the children

**Jem lops the heads of Mrs Dubose's flowers** (Chapter 11)

**Mayella Ewell attempts to seduce Tom Robinson**

Jem reads to Mrs Dubose for a month and learns a lesson in courage

**Atticus shoots the rabid dog** (Chapter 10)

Bob Ewell arrives and beats Mayella

Scout is able to 'rescue' Atticus from the lynch mob

**The children accompany Calpurnia to church** (Chapter 12)

Mayella accuses Tom of rape to excuse her behaviour

The children are able to get a seat at the trial

**Tom Robinson reveals that he felt sorry for Mayella** (Chapter 19)

**Atticus cross-examines Bob Ewell** (Chapter 17)

**Atticus proves that Tom Robinson is innocent** (Chapter 19)

This more than any other factor turns the jury against Tom

Ewell is humiliated and begins to plot revenge

**Bob Ewell spits in Atticus's face** (Chapter 17)

Tom loses all hope and is killed while trying to escape

**Mrs Grace Merriweather organises a pageant** (Chapter 27)

**Bob Ewell loses his job on the Work Projects Administration** (Chapter 27)

The children are attacked

This provides Bob Ewell with a chance to attack the children

Boo rescues Scout and Jem

GCSE English & Literature: Exam Preparation Support Pack © HarperCollins *Publishers* 2003

# To Kill a Mockingbird: Symbols

### The mockingbird

When Atticus gives his children air rifles he tells them that they can shoot all the bluejays they want, but 'it's a sin to kill a mockingbird' because mockingbirds do no harm. Boo Radley is explicitly likened to a mockingbird at the end of the novel, and it is clear that Tom Robinson and Scout herself are also 'mockingbirds' who should not be harmed.

### The Radley tree

Trees are often a symbol of life and growth. As the relationship between Boo and the children grows, Boo places gifts for them in the knot hole of a tree just inside the Radley property. Nathan Radley, who has dedicated his life to imprisoning his brother, cuts off this means of communication by filling the hole with lifeless concrete.

### The rabid dog

The self-contained episode in which Atticus shoots the rapid dog has a good deal of symbolic significance. The dog, normally a valued part of the community, has suddenly become a threat. This crisis affects everyone, black or white, rich or poor, and brings a moment of equality. Later Atticus says that the court of law has the same capability of making everyone equal, regardless of skin colour or social status. The first response to the threat is by Mr Heck Tate, the law enforcement officer, but it is finally dealt with by Atticus, the lawyer. The rabid dog itself could be regarded as a symbol of the destructive madness of racism, that eats away at a community from within.

### Mrs Dubose's morphine addiction

Mrs Dubose is an unpleasant character who shares many of the prejudices of white Maycomb society. Nevertheless she is prepared to go through appalling agonies to be 'free' of her morphine addiction before she dies. Atticus admires her determination and tells Jem that she was 'the bravest person I ever knew'. Within the novel Mrs Dubose represents bravery in the fight for freedom and provides a lesson for Scout and Jem in not judging people from appearances.

### Mr Dolphus Raymond's paper bag

In America it is illegal to drink alcohol in public; people who do so often hide what they are drinking in a paper bag. In the break from the trial Dill and Scout meet Mr Dolphus Raymond, an 'evil man' who drinks and has mixed-race children. It emerges that Mr Raymond is not a drunkard and that the bag from which he drinks contains only cola. Mr Raymond says that he pretends to drink to provide an explanation for his friendliness to black people. People can deal with odd behaviour, he says, if they have a reason to explain it. The cola inside the paper bag is a symbol of the reality that is hidden beneath appearances (see Revision Sheet 69).

### Tom's crippled arm

Tom's arm was injured in a cotton gin, a machine that was used primarily by slaves and, after emancipation, by poor black workers in the cotton fields. His damaged arm works as a plot device but it also represents the limitations placed on black people in the Southern United States. They are hindered by the legacy of slavery in everyday life, and all-white juries are incapable of admitting the significance of such injuries in court.

## Courage

Ideas about courage develop throughout the book. At first there is the childish courage required to carry out dares relating to Boo Radley; later Jem and Scout witness acts of courage concerning Atticus and the rabid dog and Mrs Dubose's fight against her morphine addiction; and finally there is the courage required to fight the Tom Robinson case.

Atticus makes it clear that he values moral courage (Mrs Dubose's) over physical courage (his own) when he says:

> *I wanted you to see what real courage is, instead of getting the idea that courage is a man with a gun in his hand. It is when you know you're licked before you begin, but you begin anyway and you see it through no matter what. You rarely win, but sometimes you do.*

Atticus defends Tom Robinson knowing he is 'licked' before he begins. In Chapter 9 Atticus tells his brother Jack, 'The jury couldn't possibly be expected to take Tom Robinson's word against the Ewells.' This was the reality of the Southern States at that time, but Atticus takes on the task because he feels he could not ask his own children to obey him or represent the town in the county legislature if he didn't.

In Chapter 15 Atticus exhibits great courage in sitting in front of the jail the night before the trial in order to protect Tom Robinson from the lynch mob. Significantly it is Scout's courage in facing up to the mob with her father that diffuses the situation.

The opposite of courage, cowardice, is a feature of Bob Ewell's behaviour. He threatens various people after the trial but is easily put off by a firm response. It is the act of a coward to attack Atticus's children rather that Atticus himself.

## Appearance and reality

The novel charts the moral development of Scout and, to a lesser extent, Jem. The most important lesson that the two children learn is that you should not judge a person by appearances. As Atticus says in Chapter 3, 'You never really understand a person until you consider things from his point of view, until you climb into his skin and walk around in it.'

This message is constantly reinforced:

- Boo Radley is a not a monster but a benevolent recluse

- Mrs Dubose's behaviour is erratic because she is fighting morphine addiction

- Mr Dolphus Raymond is only pretending to be a drunkard to provide an 'excuse' for his behaviour

- Atticus is not 'useless' but a crack shot with a rifle.

The obvious application of this message is to race. In Maycomb virtually the entire town is unable to look beyond the colour of a person's skin so that the word of a dishonest and shiftless white man is accepted over that of an honest and hard-working black man.

By the end of the novel Scout is able to see for herself that the women of Maycomb are hypocrites because they care about remote tribespeople yet cannot tolerate their own black neighbours. She is able to express the teacher's double standards about Hitler and Jews in simple but effective language: 'Jem, how can you hate Hitler so bad an' then turn round and be ugly about folks right at home – ?'

# To Kill a Mockingbird: Themes (2)

## Education

As with most novels concerning childhood, *To Kill a Mockingbird* considers the importance of education. Several sections of the novel are set in school and many of the characters are teachers of one kind or another.

**Miss Caroline** is new to Maycomb and to teaching and is an apostle of the then fashionable 'Dewey' system of education. There is a good deal of comedy at her expense as she runs into the rather strange habits of Maycomb inhabitants, but her most memorable act is to tell Scout that she should stop reading with her father because he might teach her in the wrong way. Atticus's resolution of this problem forces him to explain to Scout that there is a difference between home behaviour and public behaviour. **Miss Gates** has a current affairs lesson in which she criticises Hitler for racial prejudice without seeing the same behaviour in herself.

**Atticus** teaches, or at least allows, Scout to learn to read. He is much more concerned with his children's moral education, as is shown by his comments on Mrs Dubose. In contrast with most of Maycomb, Atticus applies the same moral standards to all his dealings. He therefore sees the trial of Tom Robinson as a moral lesson for his children. If he cannot act rightly in court he feels that he cannot ask his children to act rightly at home.

**Calpurnia** is the housekeeper and was the children's nurse who helped Scout to learn to read. Her authority is absolute when Scout is at home all the time, but it begins to diminish as Scout moves off into the world of school. When Jem and Scout go to church with Calpurnia, they see how respected she is in the local black community, and her commitment to ideals similar to those of Atticus himself.

**Aunt Alexandra** moves in with the Finches to teach Scout to be a lady. She also tries to imbue her with family pride. Apart from surface obedience, Scout largely ignores her aunt's lessons.

As well as these formal figures, the children learn lessons in life from people like Mrs Dubose, Mr Dolphus Raymond and Boo Radley. In all aspects of education in the novel it is apparent that mere authority is not important. Miss Caroline is too young herself and too influenced by the latest educational fashions to appreciate Scout's abilities and achievements, while Miss Gates is simply prejudiced. Aunt Alexandra is concerned for her niece but she what she has to say is either meaningless or irrelevant to Scout. The children learn their most valuable lessons from informal sources.

## Justice

The device of looking at Maycomb through the innocent eyes of children brings justice to its most basic level. Even quite small children have ideas of right and wrong and fair and unfair, and the Finch children assume that Tom Robinson's trial will be about these issues. Unfortunately the trial is conducted by adults and justice in its simplest sense is the last thing the trial achieves.

The first attempt at 'justice' that Scout and Jem witness is the justice of the lynch mob. The crowd that gathers outside the jail assumes that Mayella is telling the truth and that Tom Robinson should pay for committing what was then a capital offence with his life. The crowd feels that there is no need for a court procedure to establish guilt; Atticus stands up to them simply on the basis that everyone deserves a fair trial.

At the trial itself Jem assumes that the obvious truth contained in the evidence about Tom's arm will result in a just decision, and he is bitterly disappointed when this does not happen. Dill is so revolted by the way in which the trial is carried out that he is forced to leave the courthouse. In the trial itself Atticus explains that equality before the law is the highest good of a democratic society and that justice should be based on this ideal. His argument does not convince the jury but at least the time they take to convict Tom is longer than usual.

At the end of the novel Boo Radley commits the crime of manslaughter but, after consideration of who was involved and the likely consequences for society and for Boo, Heck Tate and Atticus decide that it is just to let the crime go unpunished.

Atticus believes in treating all people equally in his daily life. He also believes that we cannot treat people justly unless, to some extent, we see things from their point of view. Justice for Atticus is both a legal and a social ideal.

GCSE English & Literature: Exam Preparation Support Pack © HarperCollins *Publishers* 2003

## ◀ Prejudice

Maycomb is riddled with gender, social and racial prejudice.

### Gender prejudice

Scout hates being called a girl and thinks that the clothes Aunt Alexandra wants her to wear are 'the starched walls of a pink cotton penitentiary'. The ladies of Maycomb disapprove of Scout's nonconformity in this area: 'Well, you won't get very far until you start wearing dresses more often.' More seriously, there are no women in the juries: Jem suggests that Miss Maudie would make a better juror than the farming men from Sarum. Finally, Mayella's attempt to seduce Tom Robinson is regarded as an unforgivable sin. If she had been male or rich she might not have had to seek Tom's life in order to hide her shame.

### Social prejudice

The principal victims of social prejudice are the Ewells but we also see examples of prejudice directed at the Cunninghams and other 'poor white' families. The Ewells live almost literally beyond the pale of normal society. Bob is 'allowed' to poach out of season to feed his family, the children attend school one day a year and Mayella cannot understand what Atticus means when he asks if she has any friends.

The Cunninghams are poor but maintain their dignity by paying their way with goods or help in kind. Scout is severely criticised for making fun of Walter Cunningham's table manners, and it is a Cunningham who delays the jury's verdict at the trial. Aunt

Alexandra actively discourages Scout from mixing with the Cunninghams on the grounds that they are 'trash'.

Richer people like Atticus and Mr Dolphus Raymond have a great deal more freedom that anyone else. Atticus is not very rich but he comes from an old family. His decision to defend Tom Robinson can be forgiven on this score. Mr Dolphus Raymond is rich, but prefers black people to white. His wealth and his 'drinking' allow people to tolerate him.

At the bottom of everyone's social scale are black people. Even Bob Ewell complains about the black people living near him and damaging the neighbourhood. The black people we actually meet in the novel are uniformly hard-working and respectable. This has no effect on their social status in Maycomb.

### Racial prejudice

The chief victim of this is Tom Robinson. As Mr Link Deas points out at the trial, he is hard-working and no trouble to anyone. The crucial fact is that no white jury will accept his word over a white man's. Atticus's defence is clear and it is obvious that Tom did not commit the crime, but he is convicted anyway.

In other parts of the novel two views of the black community emerge. Through Scout, Atticus and Jem we learn of the black community's solidarity, decency and hard work. Through the ladies that Scout is forced to mix with we are told of a shiftless and sulky group of people who need to be 'put in their places'. The hypocrisy of the missionary ladies who are prepared to worry about the Mrunas tribe but not the people with whom they live and work is evident even to Scout.

## Scout (Jean Louise Finch)

### Actions

Scout narrates the book and tells of her life from about the age of six. She is a precocious tomboy who teaches herself to read even before she begins formal schooling. Scout's early adventures concern Boo Radley, as she attempts, with Jem and Dill, to make him come out. Typically her fascination with the local bogeyman turns to sympathy, and before the Boo Radley game has ended she is more concerned with communication than with scaring herself.

When Tom Robinson becomes the centre of the town's attention, Scout becomes more of a spectator, but she is not above getting into fights with her cousin and schoolfellows to defend her father's reputation, or facing up to a lynch mob. After the trial Scout becomes the object of Bob Ewell's plan for revenge on Atticus. His attack on Scout has the unintended effect of achieving the children's ambition to meet Boo.

### Role

Scout's role is that of innocent narrator. Her six-year-old view of what is right and wrong, tutored by the liberal Atticus, often runs into injustice and unfairness. The excuses that adults make for their behaviour have no hold on Scout and, through her, the reader. Her innocent eye exposes the poverty of the Cunninghams, the anomalous social position of the Ewells, the oppression of the black community, the unfairness of Tom's trial and the hypocrisy of various Maycomb ladies. The lack of adult distortion in her view enables Scout to diffuse the tension outside the jail when she simply greets one of the lynch mob, Mr Cunningham, as if nothing was out of the ordinary.

Later in the book Scout is able to see for herself the emptiness of Aunt Alexandra's claims to gentility in a town founded on alcohol and corruption. She is equally able to see that there is something wrong with a teacher who feels that Hitler's oppression of the Jews is bad when she herself represses local black people. Like Tom Robinson and Boo, Scout is one of the book's mockingbirds; the fact that she at least survives at the end of the book gives some cause for hope.

## Jem (Jeremy Finch)

### Actions

Jem is Scout's older brother and is nearly ten at the start of the novel. He is quieter and more reserved than his sister, and later in the story seems to be entering the early stages of adolescence. He joins in with Scout's games at home, and with Dill he is an enthusiastic player of the Boo Radley game, although he ignores her at school. His visit to the porch ends in near disaster and he looses his trousers as he tries to escape. Later Boo returns the trousers after attempting to repair them. Jem is particularly impressed with his father's skill with a rifle, though Atticus takes pains to point out that this skill is nothing to be proud of.

As the Tom Robinson trial takes centre stage in the story Jem tries hard to live up to his father's expectations and maintain a dignified family front. At the trial his legal knowledge and his youthful sense of fair play convince him that Tom will go free. He is deeply disappointed by the final verdict. Jem has his arm broken in the attack by Bob Ewell and this event provides the starting point of the novel.

### Role

Jem has very high expectations for himself and for other people, and he is often angry when these are not met. He often provides an emotional reaction to events that the younger, more innocent and less sophisticated Scout cannot be expected to feel, and that the ever-cautious Atticus cannot be expected to express.

## ◖ Dill (Charles Baker Harris)

### Actions

Dill's arrival as a summer visitor to Maycomb sparks off the Boo Radley game. He is a little older than Scout and they have a special relationship: Scout has a crush on him and he is regarded as her 'permanent fiancé'. He runs away from his mother and is given permission to stay in Maycomb during the summer of the Tom Robinson trial. He tends towards escapism and fantasy as a way of coping with his problems.

### Role

Dill's principal role is to act as a catalyst in the early part of the story. His interest in the Boo Radley story sparks off the Finch children's adventures and he plays an active part in many of the Boo Radley related episodes. At the trial Dill is so sickened by the way Mr Gilmer speaks to Tom that he has to leave the courtroom. Once outside his conversation with Mr Dolphus Raymond reveals his role at this point. He is told that he hasn't lost his sense of right and wrong as the adults have. His action also provides a break in tension during the trial.

## ◖ Atticus Finch

### Actions

Atticus's wife died when Scout was a baby and since then he has taken his role as the father of Scout and Jem very seriously. He has coped with bringing Jem up on his own but feels that Scout needs female support in the person of Aunt Alexandra. The early part of the novel shows Atticus as a likeable and fair man who attempts to do right both as father and lawyer. His children clearly love him, but he goes up in their estimation when he is called upon to shoot a rabid dog. Atticus is not proud of his skill with a rifle and later arranges for Jem to read to Mrs Dubose as she withdraws from morphine addiction, citing this as an example of true courage.

Atticus attempts to treat everyone equally and believes that everyone is equal in a court of law. He takes on the case of Tom Robinson out of a sense of fair play and equality, but also because he feels that if he didn't he would not be able to bring his children up properly. Before the trial takes place Atticus defends Tom Robinson from a lynch mob armed only with a standard lamp and a book. Atticus conducts the case brilliantly but its result is a foregone conclusion: no white jury will believe a black man over a white man and so Tom Robinson is found guilty. Atticus's conduct of the case arouses the resentment of Bob Ewell, the principal witness for the prosecution. Atticus ignores Bob Ewell's attempts to intimidate him until he finally attacks Jem and Scout. The children are saved by Boo Radley and Atticus agrees with Sheriff Heck Tate that it would be 'a sin' to allow Boo's role in the accidental death of Bob Ewell to become public.

### Role

Atticus is an optimist about human nature and he himself represents all that is best in the legal system. He lives according to his beliefs and attempts to treat everyone equally. This causes puzzlement and scorn amongst the rich white community but it earns him the respect of the poor whites and black people. He shows real courage in taking on the Tom Robinson case, knowing that he will lose, and he demonstrates great physical courage when he faces up to the lynch mob. After the case Atticus feels that there is some comfort to be found in the fact that the jury took five hours to bring in a guilty verdict.

As a father Atticus is less confident in his role and relies on Calpurnia, Miss Maudie and Aunt Alexandra for help. Nonetheless he does a good job of educating his two children and helping them to understand and appreciate the values he holds dear.

GCSE English & Literature: Exam Preparation Support Pack © HarperCollins *Publishers* 2003

## ◀ Boo Radley

### Actions

As a boy Boo mixed with the wrong sort of people and got into trouble with the police. His parents agreed to keep him at home rather than sending him to the state reform school. His friends were eventually released but Boo's sentence never ended. One day he stabbed his father in the leg with a pair of scissors and the family decided to continue his imprisonment, this time as an alternative to an insane asylum. By the start of the book a myth had grown up around Boo that suggested that he was some kind of monster. In fact he is simply a recluse who is too shy to leave his house.

The first part of the book relates the tale of Boo Radley and how Scout, Jem and Dill attempted to make contact with him. Their efforts to contact him are rewarded with gifts in a tree and such things as a blanket round Scout's shoulders on a cold night and the return of Jem's trousers after a dare goes wrong. Boo's brother blocks these tentative attempts at contact and Boo fades into the background of the story during the trial of Tom Robinson. At the end of the novel Bob Ewell attacks the children in the land behind the Radley house. Boo rescues the children but in the process Bob Ewell is killed. Atticus and Heck Tate agree to keep Boo's part in the rescue secret and Boo is escorted home by Scout. Here she is rewarded by the view from Boo's window which shows that he has been a benevolent watcher of her games all along.

### Role

Apart from his role in the plot, Boo's principal purpose in the novel is to teach the children not to judge by appearance and that you can't understand a person until you have walked around in his shoes.

## ◀ Tom Robinson

### Actions

Tom is a respectable and hard-working black man whose only crime seems to have been to feel sorry for Mayella Ewell. He helps her to cope with her difficult life, but when she attempts to seduce him he is forced to reject her. Firstly he is a married man, and secondly relationships between black men and white women were taboo in that time and place.

Unfortunately Mayella's attempt to kiss Tom is seen by Bob Ewell who beats his daughter savagely. She in turn is forced to accuse Tom of raping her. Tom stands trial and is ably defended by Atticus. The fact that Tom has a crippled arm proves conclusively that Tom could not have committed the rape and beating that he is accused of, but he is found guilty anyway. Atticus promises to appeal, but Tom loses hope and is shot while trying to escape.

### Role

Tom's case demonstrates the unfairness and inequality suffered by black people in the Southern states in a stark and unambiguous manner. As a person he is likeable, honest and hard-working, but this counts for nothing.

GCSE English & Literature: Exam Preparation Support Pack © HarperCollins *Publishers* 2003

# To Kill a Mockingbird: Characters (4)

## ◀ Bob Ewell

### Actions

Bob Ewell and his family make various appearances in the novel as examples of poor 'white trash'. It is clear from the evidence at Bob Ewell's trial that he beat Mayella up when he discovered her trying to kiss Tom Robinson. Neither Bob nor, it must be admitted, Heck Tate saw fit to call for medical attention for Mayella after her beating.

After the trial Bob conceives a hatred of those involved and attempts to take some sort of revenge on Judge Taylor (by prowling round his house), Helen Robinson (by following her) and Atticus (by spitting in his face). In all of these attempts he is either scared off or ignored. Atticus suggests that Bob will stop in time; instead Bob attacks the Finch children with murderous intentions. The intervention of Boo Radley results in Bob's death, but Heck Tate decides to treat the death as accidental so that Boo's peace will not be disturbed.

### Role

Bob Ewell is a pure villain. He has no shades to his character and there are no lessons for Scout and Jem to learn from him about judging from appearances; even Atticus fails to come to the right conclusions about his behaviour. Bob's role is to demonstrate the very basest aspects of white society in Maycomb. He has no job, he drinks, he fails to educate his children and he neglects them in various other ways. It is even suggested at the trial that he might have sexually abused Mayella.

Bob Ewell's example contrasts with that of respectable poor whites like Mr Cunningham and respectable black people represented by Tom Robinson, Helen Robinson and Calpurnia. In spite of his position at the bottom of the white social scale and his obvious moral inferiority to his black neighbours, Bob still looks down on black people and expects a white jury to take his word over any black man's. Unfortunately, in spite of the glaring holes in his and Mayella's testimony, he is right.

## ◀ Mayella Ewell

### Actions

Mayella Ewell is the oldest daughter of Bob Ewell. She seems to be one of the few members of the family to make an effort – she keeps herself clean and even attempts to grow flowers to brighten up her environment. Her desperate loneliness and isolation from the white community lead her to attempt to kiss Tom Robinson and, when her action is discovered by her father, to accuse Tom of raping her.

Mayella Ewell's testimony at the trial reveals how lonely she is and the lengths she had to go to get Tom Robinson alone – it took her a year to save up enough money to send her brothers and sisters out for ice-cream. Mayella is confused by Atticus's treatment of her at the trial and she has enough sense to see that her testimony is not well received. She therefore directly challenges the jury to find in her favour, accusing them of being cowards if they don't.

### Role

Mayella is more of a victim than a villain. It is clear that her 'crime' was premeditated and involved a great deal of planning and even personal sacrifice. The fact that she was prepared to do these things to achieve something that no white woman was supposed to do shows how desperately lonely and friendless she was. Nevertheless Mayella is quite prepared to see Tom Robinson executed in order to save her from any accusation of being attracted to a black man. Like her father, Mayella is at the bottom of the white social scale, but even she considers her reputation worth more than the life of a black person.

GCSE English & Literature: Exam Preparation Support Pack © HarperCollins *Publishers* 2003

# To Kill a Mockingbird: Language and style (1)

## ◀ Point of view

### A child's voice

*To Kill a Mockingbird* is presented as a memoir of events in the life of six-year-old Scout. In this kind of writing authors often reflect or comment on their younger selves, but Harper Lee avoids the temptation to include an adult voice and presents the story as if Scout were telling it at the time of the events. This is clearly impossible in terms of style, as no six- or seven-year-old could possibly write in the language that the novel is presented in. However, Harper Lee's decision to keep the 'adult voice' of Scout out of the book means that she is able to maintain her innocent point of view throughout.

The adult style is established in the opening paragraph:

> *When he was nearly thirteen my brother Jem got his arm badly broken at the elbow. When it was healed, and Jem's fears of never being able to play football were assuaged, he was seldom self-conscious about his injury.*

The word 'assuaged' is hardly the vocabulary of a six-year-old. On the other hand, Scout's childish innocence is recorded without comment or apparent irony, for example in this exchange with Dill:

> *'Scout, lets get us a baby.'*
> *'Where?'*
> *There was a man Dill had heard of who had a boat that rowed across to a foggy island where all these babies were; you could order one –*
> *'That's a lie. Aunty said God drops 'em down the chimney. At least that's what I think she said.'*
> *For once Aunty's diction had not been clear.*

This passage also casts doubt on quite how much of the rape case Scout really understood.

Sometimes the older Scout draws lessons from what she has heard – for instance, her understanding of Mayella Ewell during the court scene – and sometimes her perceptions are expressed in her seven-year-old voice. A good example of this is the conclusion Scout draws after the discussions in class about 'Old Hitler'. She notices that her teacher speaks out against Hitler's persecution of the Jews but that she had expressed satisfaction at the Tom Robinson verdict. Her comment is, 'Jem, how can you hate Hitler so bad an' then turn round and be ugly about folks right at home – ?'

### Advantages and disadvantages of this point of view

The major advantage of using Scout's narrative viewpoint is the way in which her innocence is constantly puzzled by adult hypocrisy. The disadvantage is that the reader finds out only what Scout finds out: she is the only person whose thoughts we have access to and we never know what anyone else is thinking. Equally we only see what Scout sees or is told.

The trial scene provides a good example of how Harper Lee exploits some of these advantages and disadvantages. In the first place it unlikely that a seven-year-old child would be allowed into court during a rape trial, but because of the children's visit to the First Purchase African M.E. Church, Scout and Jem have allies who provide them with a place in the balcony. Secondly Harper Lee reminds the reader that Scout is a lawyer's daughter to explain the sophisticated level of understanding that Scout and Jem display of the proceedings. Dill's lack of familiarity causes him to run out of the court during Tom Robinson's cross-examination by Mr Gilmer, neatly avoiding a second run through Tom's testimony while creating a break from the tension for the reader.

The death of Tom Robinson is almost entirely related at second hand. Scout overhears an account of Tom's death when Atticus comes to collect Calpurnia to help him tell Helen Robinson that Tom has been shot. Later Jem reports to Scout his impressions of what happened when Atticus and Calpurnia went to the Negro settlement. This is entirely believable but the episode might have been more powerfully told as a third-person narrative.

GCSE English & Literature: Exam Preparation Support Pack © HarperCollins *Publishers* 2003

# To Kill a Mockingbird: Language and style (2)

## Southern states English

Scout's speech is that of a girl growing up in 1930s Alabama and so she uses words that are not familiar outside that area, such as scuppernong (a variety of grape), haint (a ghost), collard (a type of cabbage), molasses (a sort of syrup) and chunk (to throw). Few of these words cause any difficulty in understanding the story as they tend to occur in familiar contexts and they add depth to the setting.

Atticus and the other educated adults speak something close to standard American English, although this causes some problems for Atticus at the trial when Mayella thinks that Atticus's polite mode of address is an attempt to make fun of her. Judge Taylor explains:

> *Mr Finch is always courteous to everybody. He's not trying to mock you, he's trying to be polite. That's just his way.*

Less well educated adults, children and black people speak much less formally and with a variety of local expressions:

- Mr Link Deas: *'I just want the whole lot of you to know one thing right now. That boy's worked for me eight years an' I ain't had a speck o'trouble outa him. Not a speck.'*

- Bob Ewell: *'Well, I was sayin' Mayella was screamin' fit to beat Jesus.'*

- Tom Robinson: *'I say where the chillun? ... and she says ... they all gone to town to get ice creams. She says "Took me a slap year to save seb'm nickels, but I done it."'*

- Jem: *'I declare to the Lord you're gettin' more like a girl everyday!'*

As with the unusual vocabulary, these modes of speaking add to the realism of the story. They seldom cause difficulties of understanding, given the contexts they are used in.

## Narrative technique

### Description

The most detailed description in the book is that of Maycomb in the opening chapter. After this scene-setting Harper Lee uses a mixture of description, dialogue and reflection by Scout to move the story on at a good pace. The descriptions and narrative are clearly in the voice of the adult Scout, as the following thumbnail sketches of characters demonstrate:

> *In Maycomb County, it was easy to tell when someone bathed regularly, as opposed to yearly lavations: Mr Ewell had a scalded look; as if an overnight soaking had deprived him of protective layers of dirt, his skin appeared to be sensitive to the elements. Mayella looked as if she tried to keep clean, and I was reminded of the row of red geraniums in the Ewell yard.*

> *Miss Caroline was no more than twenty-one. She had bright auburn hair, pink cheeks, and wore crimson fingernail polish. She also wore high-heeled pumps and a red-and-white striped dress. She looked and smelled like a peppermint drop.*

### Dialogue

The use of dialogue is particularly effective as it enables readers to make up their own minds about characters and their actions. This is most evident in the trial scene when Bob and Mayella condemn themselves out of their own mouths well before the evidence of Tom's arm is produced. In contrast, Boo is interesting as a character precisely because he doesn't speak. In this instance the reader has to read the clues provided by his actions, such as the gifts in the tree and the blanket placed around Scout's shoulders on the night of Miss Maudie Atkins's fire.

### Episodic structure

*To Kill a Mockingbird* was originally submitted to the publishers as a series of short stories. The present novel still bears traces of its original form in that several sections seem self-contained, such as the rabid dog episode and the story of Mrs Dubose. In addition, the Boo Radley narrative is not connected to the story of Tom Robinson, except at the end. However, even the disconnected episodes make some sort of thematic or symbolic point and therefore contribute to the whole.

GCSE English & Literature: Exam Preparation Support Pack © HarperCollins *Publishers* 2003

# The Lord of the Flies: Setting and background (1)

## About the author

William Golding was born in 1911 in Saint Columb Minor in Cornwall. He was educated at Marlborough Grammar School, where his father taught, and later at Brasenose College, Oxford, where he studied English literature and philosophy. He worked as a school teacher until he was in his fifties. In the Second World War, as an officer in the Royal Navy, he took part in the Normandy invasions and the sinking of the German battleship *Bismarck*.

*The Lord of the Flies* (1954) was Golding's first published novel. His novel *Rites of Passage* won the Booker Prize in 1980, and he received the Nobel Prize for literature in 1983. He was knighted in 1988 and died in 1993. His final novel, *The Double Tongue*, was published posthumously in 1995.

Golding has said that his view of human nature was made much darker by his experiences in the Navy. Presumably he also had plenty of time to observe the ways that boys behave during his career as a teacher.

## The literary tradition

*The Lord of the Flies* takes as a starting point the long tradition in English literature of stories set on desert islands. One of the earliest and most famous is *Robinson Crusoe* (1719), which tells the story of an Englishman surviving and prospering on a tropical island with the help, latterly, of his black companion Friday. Versions of this story for children included: *Swiss Family Robinson* (1813), in which a botanically inclined family survive and prosper on a desert island; sections of *Treasure Island* (1883), which features a marooned sailor, Ben Gunn; and *Coral Island* (1858), in which Jack, Ralph and Peterkin have a number of educative adventures on a desert island. The three thoroughly decent heroes of *Coral Island* behave impeccably throughout the novel and are rescued from savages near the end. The similarities in names alone reveal Golding's desire to comment on the absurd conclusions of a book that was written at the height of British self-confidence and pride.

## Golding's island

The map below shows the island of the novel. It is in many ways an idyllic setting, as it has enough land and vegetation to support a population of pigs, and in the lagoon and bathing pool there are sheltered areas for fishing and swimming. The map also reveals that most of the boys did not exploit its potential – only Jack and the hunters ventured into the interior on a regular basis and only Simon felt comfortable away from the beach. The boys' arrival on the island left it scarred, and on two other occasions the island was damaged extensively by fire.

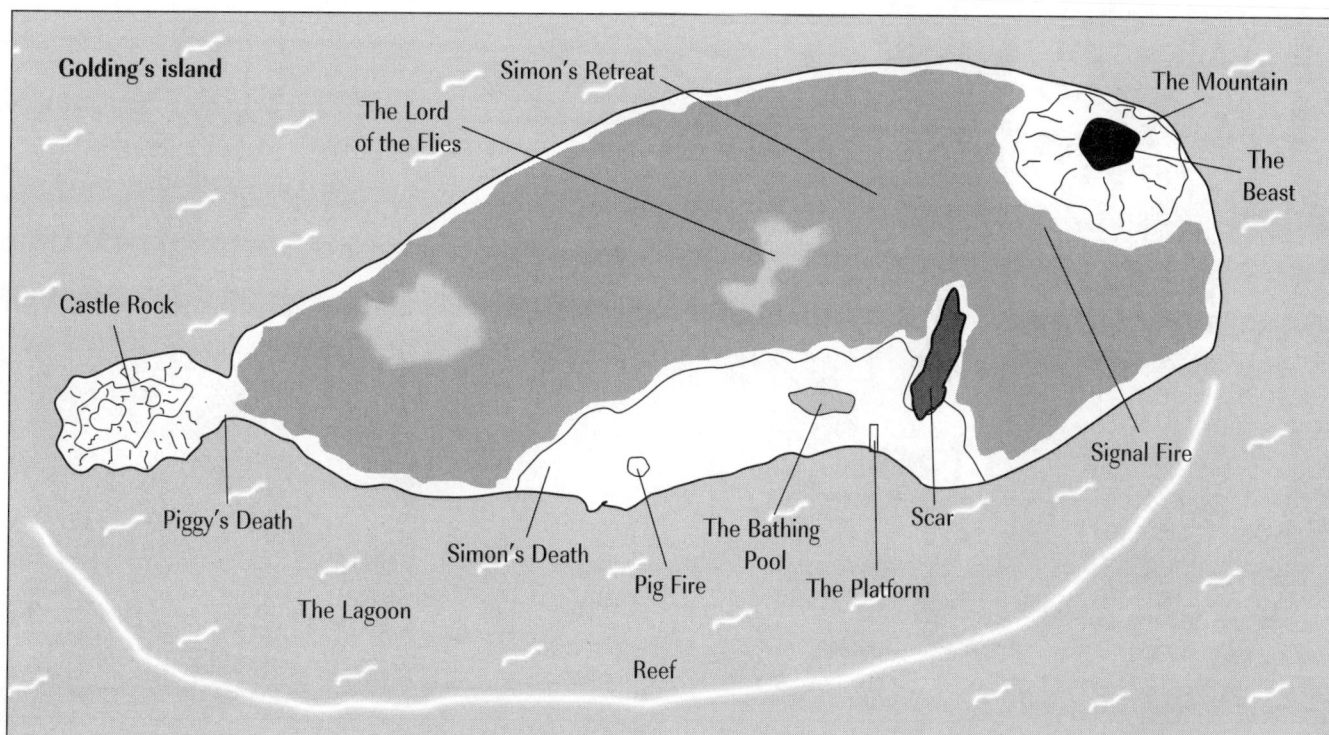

Golding's island

Labels: Simon's Retreat, The Lord of the Flies, The Mountain, The Beast, Castle Rock, Signal Fire, Piggy's Death, Simon's Death, Pig Fire, The Bathing Pool, The Platform, Scar, The Lagoon, Reef

# The Lord of the Flies:
# Setting and background (2)

## The Cold War

Aeroplanes with detachable passenger tubes did not exist in 1954 (and still do not exist) and so strictly speaking *The Lord of the Flies* is a science fiction story about a possible future nuclear war.

After the end of the Second World War Europe was divided by what Sir Winston Churchill described as an 'iron curtain'; to the east of the iron curtain was the communist bloc dominated by the USSR, and to the west were the countries of the NATO alliance dominated by the USA. Within years of the atomic bombing of Hiroshima and Nagasaki at the end of the war both sides had armed themselves with atomic weapons and a state of 'cold war' existed between the two camps.

The 1950s became a time of great international anxiety as people feared the possible outbreak of an atomic war. There is no way to defend a nation against concerted attack using atomic bombs and missiles, and so the two sides developed a policy of 'Mutually Assured Destruction' (MAD) – the country that struck first would defeat its enemy but it would itself be destroyed by a retaliatory strike. At its worst, all life on earth was threatened by this policy. There were also anxieties about atomic weapons being set off by accident or by rogue commanders. Many science fiction stories, novels and films during the 1950s explored the consequences of such a war.

Although the war in *The Lord of the Flies* is very much in the background, it is highly significant:

- The boys are present on the island because they have been evacuated to avoid bombing.

- The 'beast from the air' is a fighter pilot who has been killed in an aerial dogfight.

- The boys are rescued from the island, and the savagery they have fallen into, by a ship of war.

Golding's conclusions about the boys' ability to live in peace and harmony are coloured by his fears for the world in general in the 1950s, and by his own negative experience in the Second World War.

## The Lord of the Flies

In the Old Testament Beelzebub was a god of the Philistines (2 Kings 1:2). Beelzebub became associated with devils in general, so that in the New Testament he is called the prince of all devils (Matthew 12.24). In Milton's epic poem *Paradise Lost* he is one of the major princes of Hell, second only to Satan himself. The Hebrew term ba$^c$al zebub means literally 'the lord of flies'.

In choosing the title *The Lord of the Flies* for his novel, therefore, Golding alerts the reader that this is going to be a book about the devil.

GCSE English & Literature: Exam Preparation Support Pack © HarperCollins *Publishers* 2003

# The Lord of the Flies: Plot

### The beginning (Chapters 1–2)
War in Europe: boys are evacuated.
Their plane is shot down over a deserted tropical island.
Ralph and Piggy meet.
Ralph calls the boys with the conch.
The boys choose Ralph as their leader.
Jack is to be the leader of the hunters.
Ralph, Jack and Simon explore the island.
Ralph sets up a signal fire to attract the attention of passing ships.
They light the fire using Piggy's glasses.
The fire gets out of control.
A boy with a mulberry-coloured birthmark disappears.

### Idyllic period (Chapter 3)
The boys enjoy life without grown-ups.
Ralph has trouble maintaining the signal fire.
Building huts for shelter is difficult.

### Rescue versus the thrill of the chase (Chapter 4)
The hunters' first attempt at catching a pig.
Jack becomes obsessed with hunting.
A ship passes but the signal fire has burned out: the hunters have been on a hunt instead of watching it.
Ralph is deeply angry but Jack is euphoric from his first kill.
A ritual re-enactment of the chase.
Jack hits Piggy, breaking his glasses, for criticising his behaviour.

### The reign of the beast (Chapters 5–9)
Ralph attempts to restore order by calling a meeting.
Ralph criticises the boys about the fire.
A 'littlun' raises the issue of a beast on the island.
The older boys are unable to convince the others to think rationally.
A littlun suggests the beast hides in the sea.
An aircraft battle takes place high above the island.
A dead pilot drifts to earth on the mountain in his parachute.
Sam and Eric see the silhouette of the parachute and hear the flapping noises it makes.
They rush back to the camp and report that the beast has attacked them.
Jack and Ralph search for the beast.
It is nearly dark when they see the silhouette of the parachute.
They flee in terror.

At a meeting Jack and Ralph tell the boys what they saw.
Jack accuses Ralph of cowardice but fails to get him voted out of power.
Jack runs away, calling the hunters to join him.
Ralph instructs the remaining boys to build a new signal fire on the beach.
The mountain is abandoned to the beast.
More of the boys join Jack.
Jack becomes the chief of his own tribe.
After a successful hunt the head of the killed pig is placed on a stake in the jungle as an offering to the beast.
Simon, in a fit, speaks to the fly-covered head.
The Lord of the Flies, evil personified, tells Simon he exists within all men.
Simon sees the dead parachutist on the mountain.
Simon goes to tell the others about the parachutist and to share his insight into their fear.
When he arrives the boys are in the middle of a ritual killing of the beast; Ralph and Piggy have joined in.
They identify Simon with the beast and kill him with terrible savagery.

### Collapse (Chapters 10–12)
The following morning Piggy tries to deny his part in Simon's death; Ralph insists that they should own up to it.
Jack's hunters attack and steal Piggy's glasses.
Ralph, Piggy, Sam and Eric and a few others go to Castle Rock, Jack's stronghold.
They carry the conch and demand the return of Piggy's glasses.
Fighting follows and Roger rolls a rock onto Piggy, killing him and shattering the conch.
Ralph escapes.
Ralph hides from the hunters.
Jack tries to smoke him out.
Ralph destroys the sow's head.
He is forced out onto the beach and awaits death.

### Rescue (end of Chapter 12)
Ralph looks up to find a British naval officer who has arrived to rescue the boys.
The other boys reach the beach.
The officer asks Ralph to explain what has happened.
Ralph begins to weep, followed by the other boys.

GCSE English & Literature: Exam Preparation Support Pack © HarperCollins *Publishers* 2003

# The Lord of the Flies: Symbols (1)

## The conch

The conch is a miniature version of the island. When Ralph first finds it he appreciates its beauty, but, following Piggy's advice, it becomes the device with which Ralph calls the boys together. At first the boys are impressed by Ralph and the conch and they make up rules to govern its use. Later the conch becomes something that the boys squabble over, eventually ignore and then finally destroy. All of this is true of the island as well.

The conch also represents common sense and discipline. In their early days on the island the boys make an attempt to behave like adults and to set up rule-governed systems of behaviour. They decide that the person holding the conch has the right to speak in their meetings. As conditions deteriorate the conch is increasingly ignored until only Piggy has any respect for its symbolic value. Significantly, Jack claims that the conch does not 'count' on the mountain, the home of the fire.

Piggy takes the conch with him to make his final appeal to Jack and it is destroyed at the same time as he is killed. When the conch is smashed to pieces, the boys' last link with the rational, adult world is broken and the final hunt for Ralph begins.

## Fire

Fire is a very ambiguous symbol in the book. In the early stages it represents hope of rescue, but on the first occasion the boys build a fire it gets out of control and at least one boy, the one with the birthmark, is killed by it.

The second time the fire becomes significant is when Jack's hunters chase after a pig and let the fire go out. Here the rational scientific approach suffers a defeat at the hands of unruly passion.

Later still, as passions become murkier, the rational signal fire is replaced by the primeval cooking fire. Here the boys' passions and fears take complete control and the ritual dance round the fire precedes the killing of Simon.

Finally the boys set fire to the island during the hunt for Ralph. Here the boys' passions are out of control, as is the fire.

## Piggy's glasses

On all occasions when it is necessary to light a fire, the boys have to use Piggy's glasses, the one piece of sophisticated technology that they have available. The glasses themselves represent clear-sightedness, but they are soon broken. When the boys split into two factions, the glasses become a scarce resource that has to be struggled over; in Jack's hands they are simply a tool for making fire.

On a scientific note, Piggy is short-sighted and therefore would have worn concave lenses to correct his sight. Concave lenses cannot be used in the way that Golding describes to light a fire. This does not detract from the glasses' symbolic significance; indeed, Golding may have deliberately 'perverted' science to make his symbolic point about the perversion of technology.

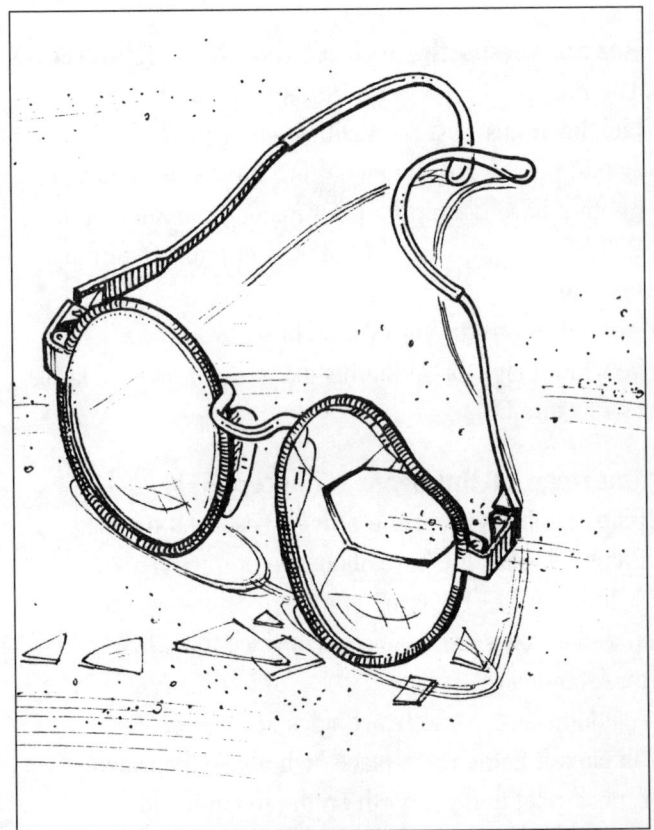

GCSE English & Literature: Exam Preparation Support Pack © HarperCollins *Publishers* 2003

## The beast

Like the fire, the beast undergoes a number of transformations in the course of the novel. The first version is the 'beastie' mentioned by the boy with the mulberry-coloured birthmark. It seems to have been the product of an overactive imagination and some large tree-creepers mistaken for snakes. Ralph immediately denies the existence of the beast but he is not old enough or experienced enough to make his denial convincing – he too suffers from night-time fears and he doesn't know enough about the sea to know if the beast is impossible.

The second major incarnation of the beast makes an explicit link between the boys' fears and the adult wars that are going on in the background of the novel. In an attempt to scotch the growing fear of the beast amongst the boys, Ralph, Jack and Roger go in search of it. What they find, in dim light, is the dead body of a fighter pilot made grotesque and fantastic by his continued connection to his parachute. The boys flee in terror and do not find out the truth about the dead man. Simon is the only person willing to face up to this beast, and he discovers its true nature on his own. He is killed before he can reveal his findings.

The third beast is also faced up to by Simon. It is the severed head of a pig set up by the boys as a sacrifice to appease their tormentor. Simon has an epileptic fit and imagines a conversation with this fly-infested monster (the Lord of the Flies of the title). In this way he comes to understand the nature of the beast itself. The boys have consistently sought to find the beast on the outside, but Simon learns that it is the inner beast, the one in the human heart, that is the real threat to everyone on the island.

The final beast is Simon. To the boys at the feast he represents the outsider, the 'other' that they fear. Ironically Simon is in a position to relieve some of their fear when he steps into their ceremony, but the message of good sense and rational investigation is drowned out by the primitive emotions that the boys have unleashed.

## The island

The island should have been a paradise. It has enough space, vegetation and food to sustain the boys, the climate is idyllic and there are no predators that could possibly threaten them. Instead the island becomes a place of torment, consumed by flames and ruled over by the Lord of the Flies – in short, hell.

The boys' arrival on the island scars it, and the longer they stay the more damage they do to it. *The Lord of the Flies* was written before concern for the environment became fashionable, but Golding clearly intends to make the boys' treatment of the island stand for humanity's treatment of the planet.

## Painted faces

There is a rational reason for a hunter to wear face paint, as it can help him to blend into the background, but when Jack and the others begin to wear face paint it represents a major step away from their old, civilised selves. The masks they adopt help them to take on new personas and liberate them from their old selves.

## Roger's stone throwing

In the episode where Roger throws stones near Henry as he plays on the beach there is an invisible circle around the younger boy into which Roger will not throw the stones. This circle represents the influence of adults and civilisation on Roger. By the end of the novel its power has disappeared: it is Roger who unleashes the rock that kills Piggy.

*See Revision Sheets 84–86 for the symbolic significance of the major characters.*

### The nature of civilisation

The central theme of the book is an exploration of the idea of human nature and human civilisation. Inspired, or rather dismayed, by novels that show people adapting to life on a desert island by simply importing their old values and modes of existence, Golding attempts to look at what would really happen if the forces that hold civilisation together were suddenly removed.

His conclusion is a pessimistic one. Civilised behaviour, it seems, is a hard-won discipline that must be constantly reinforced in order to hold back darker and more basic passions. Without the controlling presence of adults and the restraining influence of habit, the boys on the island prove incapable of realising the promise of the paradise they have been handed. Ralph and Piggy represent the decent, adult-orientated view of the world that the boys aspire to, but neither character is able to deal with the fundamental problem of the beast. Rational Piggy simply dismisses it, while Ralph tries to bring good sense to bear. However, as Simon learns in his conversation with the Lord of the Flies, these approaches cannot solve a problem that is buried deep within the human heart.

The beast represents the fear that all civilisations must conquer if they are to survive, the fear of the outsider, of others and, indeed, fear of one's own impulses that are normally masked and hidden. The boys on the island fail to deal with their fear and turn away from science and reason towards ritual and magic. They mask their bodies in order to hide their vulnerabilities and they attack any of the original group who attempts to stand outside their new 'order'.

Golding could have left the story as an interesting speculation on how boys might behave on a desert island, but by delivering them to the island on an aeroplane escaping from a nuclear war, inflicting a dead fighter pilot 'beast' on them and rescuing them on a warship he makes it clear that the boys are only acting out a miniature version of the adult world. In the aftermath of two world wars and in the shadow of the Cold War, Golding suggests that fear, and the desperate behaviour needed to conquer it, are built into the human heart and that war is an almost inevitable by-product of human society.

### Political allegory

The Second World War was seen by many as a conflict between dictatorship and democracy, and the Cold War adopted the same rhetoric. Fascist dictatorships such as those of Hitler and Mussolini were agreed to be efficient but brutal. (It was frequently said of Mussolini before the war that 'at least he made the trains run on time'.) Democracies, on the other hand, were an inefficient 'least bad' method of government that allowed individual freedom and intellectual progress.

The contrast between dictatorships and democracies is enacted in the novel. Ralph and Piggy represent the rational and democratic approach to running society, while Jack and Roger represent the effective but brutal dictatorship. In Golding's view neither side is completely good nor completely bad, but the balance of good over evil generally comes out in democracy's favour. Unfortunately democracy does not work well in a fear-induced crisis, and the book casts doubts on whether the Western democracies can survive in the Cold War world.

### Loss of innocence

This is what Ralph weeps for at the end of the novel. The boys' descent from well-behaved, well-dressed schoolboys and choirboys to face-painted savages is certainly extreme, but Golding suggests that this loss of innocence would have happened anyway. One of the things that adults protect children from is themselves, and in the absence of adults on the island the boys are forced to confront their own natures rather more rapidly than normal. Some characters, like Piggy, have a blinkered view of reality which they are able to maintain throughout the novel, but others must face up to their own fears and instincts for power, destructiveness and savagery. After Simon is killed Piggy tries to deny that he and Ralph were involved, but Ralph insists that they were there and that they were as responsible for the murder as anyone else.

GCSE English & Literature: Exam Preparation Support Pack © HarperCollins *Publishers* 2003

## Ralph

### Actions

Ralph is the first character we meet and his thoughts on his experiences end the book. At the beginning of the story we see him taking simple delight in his surroundings, but he soon meets Piggy who encourages him to blow the conch and call the other boys together. This act leads to Ralph becoming the leader of the boys without his actively seeking the position. Significantly, at this early stage of the novel, Ralph betrays Piggy by revealing his hated nickname to the group.

Having become leader, Ralph takes his duties seriously and sets about exploring the island, building shelters for the boys and making provisions for their rescue. None of his schemes is very effective as Ralph lacks both the temperament to force the other boys to do as he wants and the maturity to deal adequately with their fears. He fails most completely in his response to the problem of the beast; he is not quite old enough to dismiss the littluns' fear of this creature out of hand, and when he does go in search of the beast he has the misfortune of encountering the dead airman and his parachute in a dim light.

Ralph becomes increasingly incapable of keeping meetings under control. When Jack sets up his own group, offering the boys meat and protection from the beast, Ralph has nothing to offer the boys with him other than more of the same muddling through and hope of rescue. After the feast Ralph is with the group that kills Simon, and after the death of Piggy he becomes a victim of Jack's ruthless campaign to rid the island of 'others'.

### Role

As the central character Ralph is clearly meant to be regarded sympathetically, but he betrays Piggy at the outset, leads the boy poorly in the middle of the story and is one of Simon's killers near the end. The crucial test of Ralph's character is his response to these events. We experience his delight at the near paradise he finds himself in and we witness his confusion as his good intentions come to nothing. Unlike Piggy he does not attempt to deny his part in Simon's death and at the end of the novel Ralph weeps for the loss of innocence and the death of a dear true friend. Ralph thus represents an ordinary decent person thrown into an extraordinary situation. He is by no means perfect, but we can feel sympathy for him and wish him well because of his honesty and integrity.

On a symbolic level Ralph represents the Western democracies that struggled in the Second World War and in the Cold War. Golding sees these forms of government as less than efficient, but they are generally on the side of the angels and they attempt to be decent.

# The Lord of the Flies: Characters (2)

## Jack Merridew

### Actions

Jack is a natural leader, as his appearance at the head of a disciplined group of choirboys makes clear from the very start. He is clearly ambitious and therefore disappointed when he is not chosen to lead the whole group of boys on the island. He preserves a power base, however, by instantly reclassifying his choirboys as hunters and firewatchers. Ralph likes Jack at first and is keen to cooperate with him – they go on the first expedition to explore the island together – but Jack's very different set of priorities soon leads to conflict.

At Jack's first attempt to kill a living thing he cannot do it – he has to master himself in this area before he can lead the others – but once he has learned the thrill of the chase he becomes obsessed with hunting. This leads to his first major conflict with Ralph, when the hunters let the fire go out, and it also reduces Jack's desire to actually escape from the island. His discovery of face paint also helps to distance himself from his old self.

As fear of the beast comes to dominate the lives of the boys on the island, Jack is able to consolidate his power base and eventually take control. He does this by solving the beast problem symbolically – first by presenting the sow's head as an offering to the malign forces that trouble the island and secondly by 'killing' the beast in a ritual manner. Unfortunately Simon's arrival at the height of the ritual makes a symbolic act a real one. Once in charge Jack's latent cruelty becomes more obvious and he begins torturing boys for no very obvious reason other than power and self-gratification. In the final stages of the book he attempts to remove Ralph, the last outsider and his former rival, from the island.

### Role

Jack is the villain of the novel, but like many evil things he is not unattractive. He commands the loyalty of the choir through fear and he is enthusiastic, at first, about having lots of rules. It is when the rules affect Jack's pleasure that he becomes difficult. We see his progress from squeamishness to savagery and outright cruelty, but we can understand his desire to do something about the problem of the beast. When he gains power he seems to be far more effective than Ralph at getting things done, though at the expense of freedom and choice for the boys.

Politically Jack resembles any number of dictators who have used the army as a power base and stamped their authority on the civilian population. Although he seems to represent order, Jack in fact releases chaos on the island. His use of fire to catch Ralph threatens to destroy the entire island environment, just as the militaristic dictators of the 1950s threatened to destroy the earth with their weapons.

GCSE English & Literature: Exam Preparation Support Pack © HarperCollins *Publishers* 2003

## ◖ Piggy

### Actions

Piggy is the second person that we meet on the island. He is much less superficially attractive than Ralph, being overweight and self-conscious about his body, and, we learn, he is much less inclined to make an effort than Ralph, claiming that his asthma debilitates him. Piggy instantly seizes on Ralph as an ally and confides his hated nickname to him. Piggy suffers Ralph's betrayal in this matter patiently and he remains Ralph's loyal lieutenant throughout the rest of the story.

Piggy's glasses prove to be the only means of starting a fire on the island but they do not give him any status with the likes of Jack. The glasses are soon broken in a struggle with Jack and eventually Jack and his hunters steal them. In most of the novel Piggy tries to organise the younger boys and is a staunch defender of order (represented by the conch) and the adult point of view. Like Ralph, however, he takes part in the death of Simon, though he tries to deny this later. The death of Piggy under a rock dislodged by Roger marks the end of any attempt at maintaining a civilised society on the island.

### Role

Piggy, in spite of his glasses, is the only boy who remains clear-sighted about their goals. He constantly supports Ralph in his efforts to secure rescue from the island and he is the most consistently 'adult' of all the boys. He is not, however, without his faults. He seems to be physically lazy and he is prepared, at the feast, to prefer his stomach over his principles. After Simon's death he pretends that he and Ralph were not involved. Nevertheless he is a true friend to Ralph and his death is genuinely shocking and distressing.

On a political level Piggy represents the scientific community. The ownership of technology is thought to be a good thing in itself and scientists, Golding suggests, are naive if they think that their inventions won't be used by the dictators of this world for their own selfish ends.

## ◖ Simon

### Actions

Simon's first appearance in the novel marks him as an outsider. His epilepsy causes him to faint and the other boys think he may be mad. He is, however, chosen to explore the island with Jack and Ralph, and as the novel progresses he is the only person who feels comfortable in the deep jungle. He is helpful in practical matters but his diffidence and stammer mean that he has little impact in meetings.

When Jack, Roger and Ralph flee from the dead pilot, Simon has the courage to face up to whatever had terrorised his friends. He also has enough insight to understand the message of the Lord of the Flies. He dies with his message of hope undelivered, but the description of his body being washed out to sea implies a kind of personal redemption for Simon.

### Role

Simon represents a more spiritual and introspective aspect of human nature than either Piggy or Ralph, though he is ignored or ostracised by the group because of this. Simon's death in the service of the group invites comparisons with Jesus, but in Golding's pessimistic view of the world the message he has to offer is undelivered. Instead of bringing redemption, Simon's death signals the moral bankruptcy of Ralph and Piggy and marks the slide into savagery of Jack and Roger.

## ◖ Roger

### Actions

Roger goes unregarded in the early stages of the novel, but as civilised behaviour amongst the boys declines Roger comes into his own. He begins by acts of petty thuggery such as kicking over other boys' sandcastles, and works his way to murder. Early on in the novel he is still inhibited enough by education and habit not to throw stones directly at people. Unhappily for Piggy his inhibitions have disappeared by the time he unleashes the rock that kills him.

### Role

Roger illustrates the simple truth that evil times encourage evil people. In a well-regulated society he is unremarkable, but in an anarchy his grasp on morality is so slim that he is capable of killing without a great deal of thought or compunction.

GCSE English & Literature: Exam Preparation Support Pack © HarperCollins *Publishers* 2003

# The Lord of the Flies: Language and style (1)

## Point of view

*The Lord of the Flies* uses a third-person 'omniscient' point of view. This means that Golding is free to report on the actions, thoughts and feelings of any character in the novel. The main character is Ralph, with whom we begin and end the book and about whom we learn most, but there are sections in which Jack, Simon, Piggy, Roger and even Sam and Eric are at the centre of our attention.

## Narrative technique

Events in the novel progress in a linear manner, and there are few references, even in the dialogue, to the past. We learn most about Piggy, who is most attached to the world the boys have left behind; for example, we are given details about his asthma and his auntie. We find out little about Ralph other than the fact that his father is in the navy and that he once lived in a cottage on the moors. We can deduce that Jack and his group were in a choir before they arrived. Simon and Sam and Eric all remember a teacher called 'Waxy'. We learn Percival's address and telephone number even if he forgets these details himself before the end of the narrative. The point that Golding seems to be making by providing so few details is that the boys themselves live mostly in the present once they are on the island; their pasts are irrelevant to the roles they adopt when they are there.

Time passes on the island: the boys' hair grows long and most of their clothing seems to fall apart. However, Golding provides no clear chronology. Piggy is gently ridiculed when he comes up with his sundial idea and none of the boys, not even Piggy or Ralph, seems to think it important to keep a track of how much time has passed. They are either too involved in their own present, like the littluns and Jack, or focused on possible future rescue, like Ralph and Piggy.

## Accent and dialect

A great deal of the action and meaning of the novel is communicated through dialogue. Most of the boys seem to be from middle-class backgrounds and speak unaccented standard English. They use some slang terms, such as 'windy' for scared and 'waxy' for angry, but generally they are 'well spoken'. Even when the boys are being crude they do not quite use rude words; they stick the pig 'up the ass' rather than the more usual English term. The one occasion on which 'bad' language is used is therefore doubly shocking: Jack's 'Bollocks to the rules!' breaks the rules of language as well as the rules of the assembly.

The single exception to the boys' standard English dialect is Piggy. His lower middle-class accent marks him out as different from the other boys from the very beginning. They make fun of his 'ass-mar' throughout the novel, and Jack in particular seems to discount everything he says from the very beginning.

## Pace

Golding varies the pace of his narrative according to circumstance. In the following sentences he slows down the pace by adding detail after detail and clause after clause:

> *The first rhythm that they became used to was the slow swing from dawn to quick dusk. They accepted the pleasures of morning, the bright sun, the whelming sea and sweet air, as a time when play was good and life so full that hope was not necessary and therefore forgotten.*

In the final chase, however, the sentences become as jagged and fragmented as Ralph's thoughts:

> *Break the line.*
> *A tree.*
> *Hide, and let them pass.*

GCSE English & Literature: Exam Preparation Support Pack © HarperCollins *Publishers* 2003

# The Lord of the Flies: Language and style (2)

## Foreshadowing

A number of ideas and scenes occur more than once, so that comparisons with earlier or later events can be made. Piggy's death, for instance, is foreshadowed by the account of Roger throwing stones around but not at Henry, and by the account of the dislodging of the big rock on the boys' first visit to Castle Rock. The recurring meetings provide an obvious index for the reader of the boys' slide into chaos, and there is a striking contrast between Ralph, Jack and Simon's initial optimistic exploration of the island and their fearful search for the beast. Similarly there are two major fires and two ships that pass the island, and two references to a stick sharpened at both ends.

## Describing death

There are three deaths on the island. The first is accidental and merely shocking. When Piggy notices that the boy with the mulberry-coloured birthmark is missing the boys are briefly silent.

Simon's death is utterly savage. The crowd of boys acts like a single savage animal:

> At once the crowd surged after it, poured down the rock, leaped onto the beast, screamed, struck bit tore. There were no words, and no movements but the tearing of teeth and claws.

Simon is dehumanised by being referred to as 'it'. The death is followed by a cleansing rain storm which also frees the island from the presence of the dead airman.

The description of Simon's dead body being washed out to sea surrounded by luminescent forms takes away some of the horror of Simon's death and suggests that he at least has been absorbed by a bigger, brighter and better world. In the final paragraph of Chapter 9 Golding evokes an almost cosmic view:

> Somewhere over the darkened curve of the world the sun and moon were pulling; and the film of water on the earth planet was held, bulging slightly on one side while the solid core turned. The great wave of the tide moved further along the island and the water lifted. Softly, surrounded by a fringe of inquisitive bright creatures, itself a silver shape beneath the steadfast constellations, Simon's dead body moved out towards the open sea.

The alliteration of 's' here also has a calming effect.

The death of Piggy combines the two contrasting elements of Simon's death with the silence that followed the death of the boy with the birthmark:

> Piggy fell forty feet and landed on his back across that square, red rock in the sea. His head opened and stuff came out and turned red. Piggy's arms and legs twitched a bit, like a pig's after it has been killed. Then the sea breathed again in a long, slow sigh, the water boiled white and pink over the rock; and when it went, sucking back again, the body of Piggy was gone.

> This time the silence was complete. Ralph's lips formed a word but no sound came.

The cleansing effect of the sea is telescoped together with the harsh brutality of the death itself, the comparison with a dying pig reflects the boys' experience of killing, and the fact that it is only Ralph that tries to break the silence shows how inured to death the boys have become.

# Approaching non-fiction and media texts

Reading non-fiction and media texts is a little more complex than responding to a poem or a novel, as there are usually more things to take into account. The basic questions that you need to ask are:

**Who produced the text and for what purpose?** With a novel or poem you know more or less who produced it and why, though some poems and novels have purposes beyond entertainment. Your response to a media text, however, will be different if you are looking at an advertisement as opposed to a public information leaflet. Similarly, you might be more suspicious of the things you read in an advertisement (purpose: to sell you something) than in a newspaper (purpose: to tell you something).

- Give an example of a media text producer. What is its purpose?
- Can the same text have more than one purpose? Give examples.

**What genre does the text belong to?** Media texts come in many forms and we are generally very good at working out the 'rules' of particular texts. We are happy to watch soap operas that have several stories running at once, but we would find an information leaflet that tried to tell us about heart disease and the beauties of rural Wales frustrating and confusing.

- Can you name three media genres?
- How are the 'rules' of a newspaper story different from the 'rules' of a short story?

**Who is the audience for the text?** This is a very important question as media texts are often aimed at very specific audiences. You only have to think of the front covers of a few magazines to realise how images and words are skilfully manipulated to attract the attention of different groups. When commenting on a poem we are interested in the words themselves; when we comment on a media text we need to think how the words or images have been tailored for their audience.

- What colours would you use if you were aiming a text at small children?
- What would you assume about a product if it was advertised using images of exotic foreign locations?

**How does the text create meaning?** Newspaper stories are organised differently from information leaflets, and feature films have a different set of rules to television advertisements. Again, we tend to be good at knowing how different texts work and use these features to our advantage. Some people, for instance, always begin reading newspapers at the back where the sports news is.

- How can you usually tell the villain in an old-fashioned Western?
- What do you usually notice first on a roadside poster – the picture or the words? Why?

**How is the text produced?** The way a text is produced can affect how you view it. A product advertised with an expensive, full-colour poster will be seen differently from one advertised on a handwritten billboard. Images in black and white which could have been reproduced in colour tell us about a decision that the producers have made and provide insight into what they are trying to achieve.

- Why might an advertisement in a full-colour magazine use an image in black and white?
- Why do you think some newspapers use a tabloid format, others a broadsheet? What message does the format give?

**How does the text present its subject?** The way in which certain subjects are represented in the media can provide a great deal of information about the assumptions of the media producers. For instance, in the 1950s it was assumed that most men worked and most women stayed at home, looked after the children and did the housework. In the present century advertisers or television programme producers would soon be criticised if all they showed was this type of family.

- Do you think reality TV programmes really reflect reality?
- Do you get annoyed if all the important characters in a film or TV programme are male?

# Analysing a media text

Below is a typical media text. It could be part of a newspaper page or it could be taken from a magazine or leaflet.

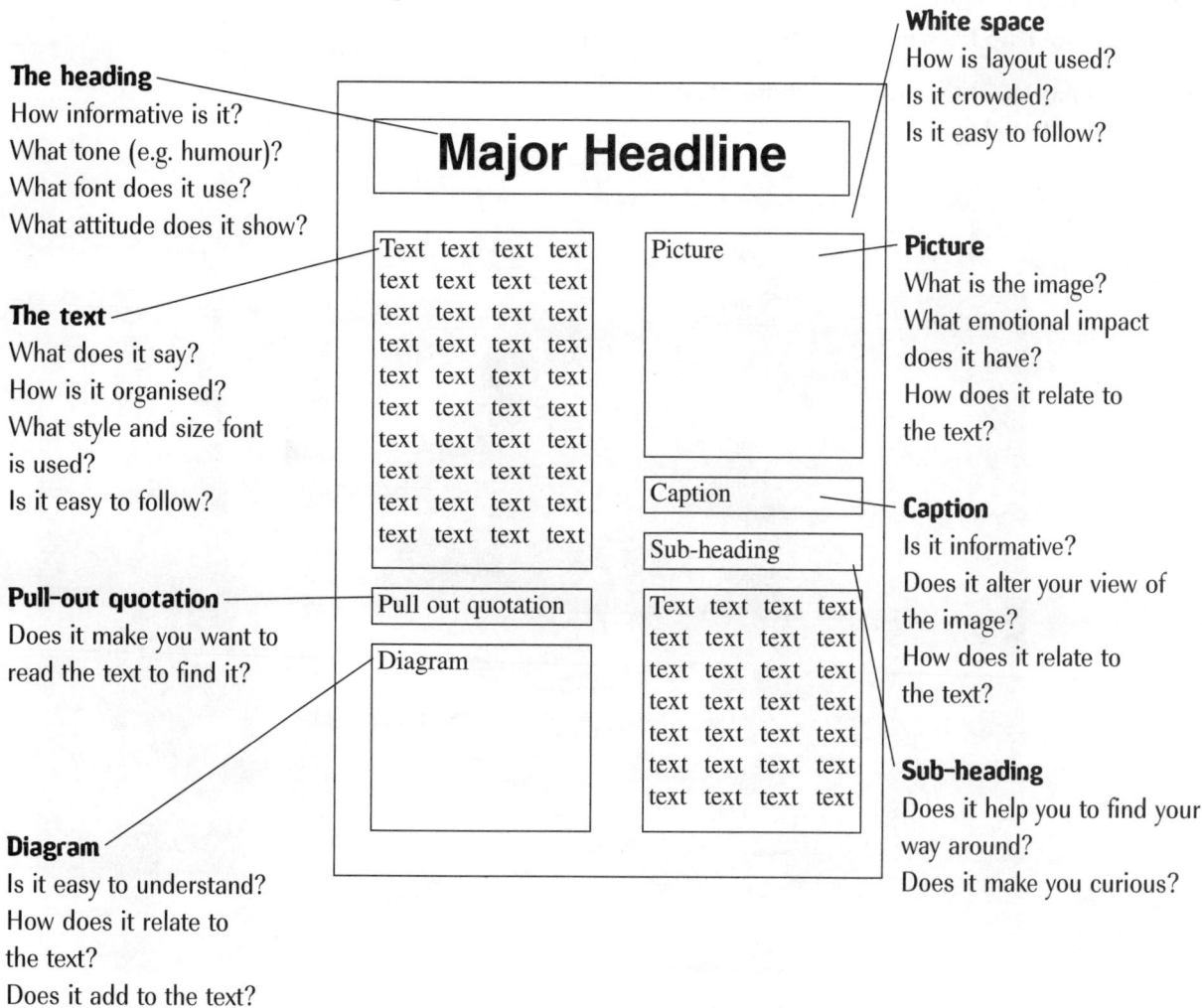

**White space**
How is layout used?
Is it crowded?
Is it easy to follow?

**The heading**
How informative is it?
What tone (e.g. humour)?
What font does it use?
What attitude does it show?

## Major Headline

Text text text text
text text text text
text text text text
text text text text
text text text text
text text text text
text text text text
text text text text
text text text text
text text text text

Picture

**Picture**
What is the image?
What emotional impact
does it have?
How does it relate to
the text?

**The text**
What does it say?
How is it organised?
What style and size font
is used?
Is it easy to follow?

Caption

Sub-heading

**Caption**
Is it informative?
Does it alter your view of
the image?
How does it relate to
the text?

**Pull-out quotation**
Does it make you want to
read the text to find it?

Pull out quotation

Diagram

Text text text text
text text text text
text text text text
text text text text
text text text text
text text text text
text text text text

**Sub-heading**
Does it help you to find your
way around?
Does it make you curious?

**Diagram**
Is it easy to understand?
How does it relate to
the text?
Does it add to the text?

1 With a partner discuss the questions surrounding the media text. What would you say was the main purpose of each of the different elements of the page?

2 Share your ideas with the rest of the class.

3 Choose a full-page advertisement from a magazine or newspaper and make notes on the following points:

- What image is used?
- What does the image say about the thing advertised?
- What text is used?
- How does the text affect your response to the image?
- What devices, if any, are used to make the text interesting or memorable?
- Is there a slogan?
- Is there a company logo? If so, why do you think it is present?

# Responding to non-fiction and media texts in the exam (1)

Below and on page 99 are two posters, a newspaper article and a mock exam question.

1 Before looking at the exam questions, study the three texts with a partner,
using the questions we have been asking in this section so far (page 96).

2 Share your conclusions about the posters with the class.
Were your opinions affected by the article?

**Poster 2**

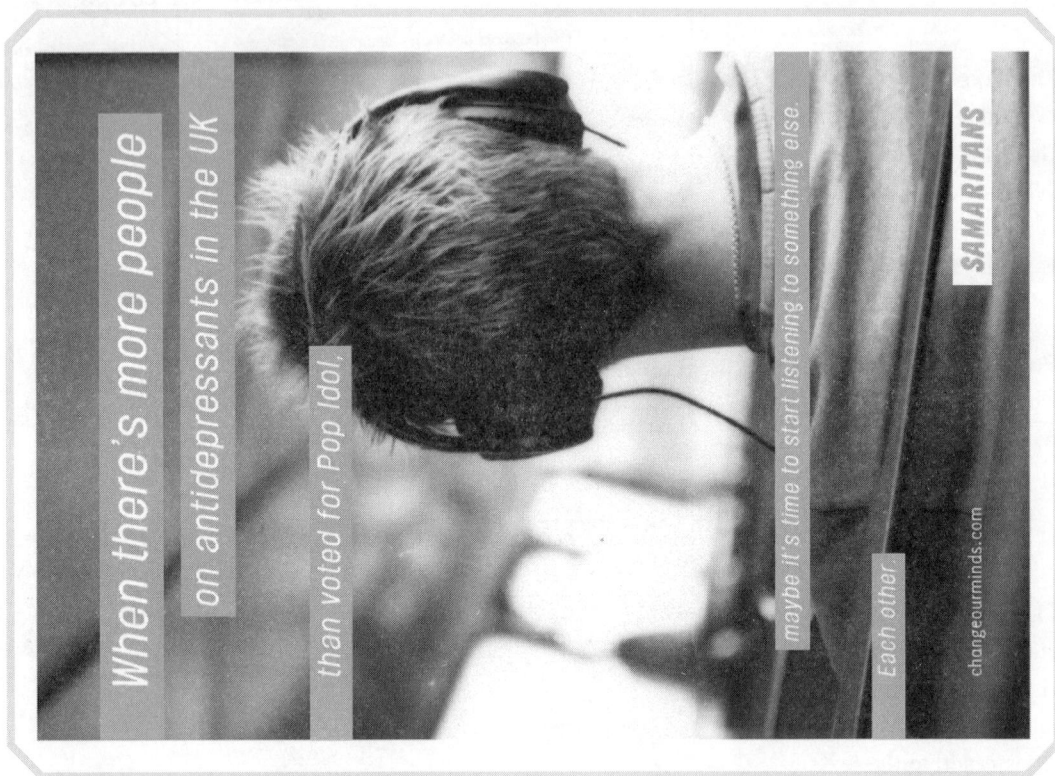

When there's more people on antidepressants in the UK than voted for Pop Idol, maybe it's time to start listening to something else. Each other. SAMARITANS changeourminds.com

**Poster 1**

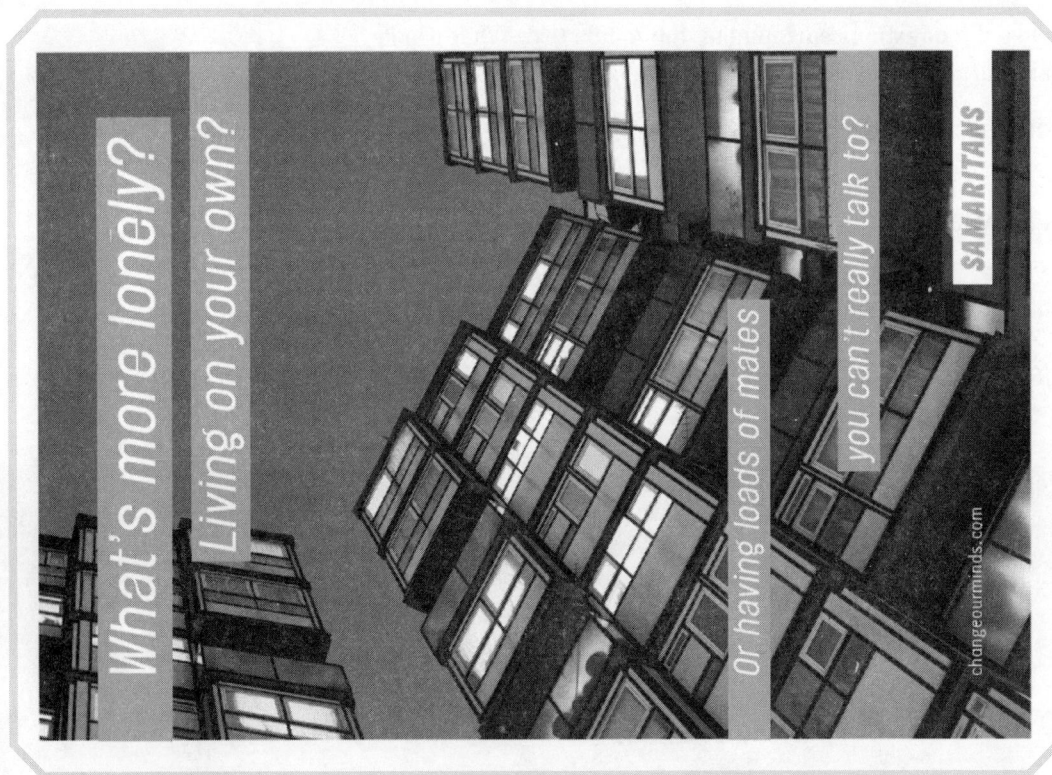

What's more lonely? Living on your own? Or having loads of mates you can't really talk to? SAMARITANS changeourminds.com

GCSE English & Literature: Exam Preparation Support Pack © HarperCollins *Publishers* 2003

# Branded for life

## *Samaritans' new image to reflect its wide-ranging role*

Raekha Prasad
Wednesday October 2, 2002
*The Guardian*

The Samaritans is today "re-branding" for the first time in its 50-year history, in a bid to increase donations and boost volunteer numbers.

Research for the charity found that while 90% of the public was aware of its existence, few people could accurately describe its service. Many respondents said the charity simply supported people when they were suicidal.

However, the Samaritans says it provides support to people across the emotional spectrum – not only those who are suicidal – and it is "repositioning" itself to improve public understanding of its role.

The Samaritans' 18,300 volunteers are being briefed about the re-branding, which has been developed by consultancy Wolff Olins and includes amending the charity's name to simply "Samaritans". A poster and press campaign will be launched next month.

Simon Armson, the charity's chief executive, says there is a perception that people's problems have to be extreme before they contact a Samaritan. "We're making it clear that suicide reduction remains very central to our philosophy, but that people may not be actively suicidal to need hope and support," he says. "Samaritans is to do with coping and finding a way forward. That's what we've always been."

The re-branding also aims to expand the organisation's donor base. Armson says: "I hope that more people will want to donate to us and see that we are relevant. If they can see the organisation more clearly in its context, then hopefully it will be more attractive to them."

In addition to the charity's 24-hour telephone service, Samaritans volunteers provide emotional health education, with many going into schools. Last month, the charity announced it was to work closely with rural organisations to raise awareness of emotional and financial support in countryside areas.

## Mock Question

1 You are being asked to follow an argument, select material appropriate to their purpose and distinguish between fact and opinion.

   Read the two Samaritan posters.

   a  What opinions are implied by Poster 1?                                                  (2 marks)

   b  What fact is communicated in Poster 2?                                                  (2 marks)

   c  Which poster gives a better idea of what Samaritans are about?                          (6 marks)

   Now read the article from The Guardian, 'Branded for life'.

   d  Explain in your own words the main purpose of the re-branding of Samaritans.            (6 marks)

2 You are now being asked to read the texts as media texts.

   a  Discuss the different approaches taken by the writing on the two posters.               (4 marks)

   b  How do the images on the two posters help to communicate their ideas?                   (4 marks)

   c  What techniques does the newspaper article use to get and hold its
      readers' attention?                                                                     (3 marks)

<br><br><br>

# Responding to non-fiction and media texts in the exam (3)

## Planning and structuring your response

The exam features two questions:

- The first question is to test your understanding of the text and your ability to select material.
- The second question asks you to respond to the materials provided as media texts.

The examiners provide you with guidance on how much to write by telling you how many marks are available for each question. Use this information wisely: for example, do not spend too long on any answer which carries only one or two marks.

For the first question make sure you know the difference between fact and opinion. It is essential to use quotations or close references to the text in this part of the paper.

For the second question try to think about the impact of the document you have studied as a whole. Remember the basic questions that you should ask about media texts, as discussed on page 96.

## Analysing sample responses

1 How many marks out of 6 would you give to the following response to question 1d? Discuss the response with a partner. How might it be improved?

> The main purpose of re-branding Samaritans is to help people to understand better what the organization does. Most people have heard of Samaritans but not many people are clear about what services it provides. The charity has changed its name slightly to draw attention to itself and it is hoping to use a poster campaign to show people that it does more than cope with suicides. When people are aware of this it is hoped that more people will donate money.

2 How many marks out of 3 would you give to the following response to question 2c? How might this response be improved?

> The most obvious way in which the article gets it reader's attention is through the headline. The words 'Branded for Life' do not tell you anything about the story but it makes it sound interesting or possibly cruel. When you read the story you realise the headline is a pun that could mean 'marked for life' or 'given a new image to help with saving lives'. The story itself is told quickly and efficiently in the first three paragraphs. The first part of the story gives the facts but not in much detail. The last part of the story has some long quotations so that readers who want to know more can find out further details from the people concerned.

## Over to you ...

Now answer all the questions set. Remember that you are advised to spend no more than 1 hour on this section of the paper.

# Writing to argue

The writing to argue question in the exam requires you to show awareness of the following:

- The **purpose** of the writing – how well can you present an argument? Can you present your ideas clearly in a way that readers can follow? Can you anticipate possible objections to your argument? Can you make your argument compelling by using such things as facts, figures, emotive language and rhetorical devices?
- The **audience** – is your argument presented in a way that will appeal to its target audience?
- The **format** – are you aware of the conventions, such as headlines, bullet points or addresses, of the kind of writing you have been given? How well do you use these conventions?

> ## Mock Question 1
>
> Write an article for a magazine aimed at teenagers. In it you should **argue** the case for talking more as a way of dealing with problems.

## Planning and structuring your response

You should begin by identifying the audience, format and purpose of the task, and make some notes on what each aspect will require. Here are the notes made by one student:

Audience - Teenagers. Informal friendly style. Informal language.

Format - Magazine article. Include headline. Subheadings?

Purpose - Argue for more talking. Talking about feelings, not football or TV. Finding right person to talk to. Importance of listening. Finding time and place to talk. Consequences of not talking. Clear structure.

Read through these notes with a partner. How might they be improved?

## Analysing a sample response

Sample Response 1 on page 108 is the start of an answer to the question. Read it and think about the following issues:

- Does it show an understanding of audience, format and purpose?
- Does it communicate clearly and imaginatively?
- Are the ideas organised well into sentences and paragraphs?
- Are a range of sentence structures used effectively, with accurate punctuation and spelling?

Refer to the examiner's mark scheme on page 107 and discuss with a partner what grade you think it might achieve. Highlight on the sample response where the assessment criteria are fulfilled.

## Over to you ...

Now answer the question yourself. Can you improve on the example?

Spend no more than 45 minutes on your answer. Remember to spend 5 minutes planning and sequencing your material before you begin writing, and 5 minutes checking your paragraphs, punctuation and spelling at the end.

GCSE English & Literature: Exam Preparation Support Pack © HarperCollins *Publishers* 2003

# Writing to persuade

The writing to persuade question in the exam requires you to show awareness of the following:

- The **purpose** of the writing – how well can you persuade your audience? What techniques, such as carefully chosen facts and figures, emotive language and rhetorical devices, are you able to use? Are you able to appeal to the thoughts and feelings of your audience?
- The **audience** – will the persuasive devices appeal to your target audience? Are your ideas expressed in an appropriate language and style?
- The **format** – have you made use of the conventions of the type of writing you have been given, such as headlines, bullet points or diagrams, to make your points as persuasively as possible?

---

### Mock Question 2

Your school is thinking of introducing a school counselling service, so that students will have someone other than friends, parents or teachers to help them discuss their problems.

Write a letter to the chair of governors at your school to **persuade** the governors to support the introduction of the service.

---

## ◖ Planning and structuring your response

You should begin by identifying the audience, format and purpose of the task, and make some notes on what each aspect will require. Here are the notes made by one student:

> Audience - Board of governors. Adults. Serious issue. Formal style and language.
>
> Format - Letter. Formal layout. Address, date. Start 'Dear Chair of Governors'. End 'Yours sincerely'.
>
> Purpose - Persuasion. Emotive language. Facts and figures, examples. Clear structure.

Read through these notes with a partner. How might they be improved?

## ◖ Analysing a sample response

Sample Response 2 on page 108 is the start of an answer to the question. Read it and think about the following issues:

- Does it show an understanding of audience, format and purpose?
- Does it communicate clearly and imaginatively?
- Are the ideas organised well into sentences and paragraphs?
- Are a range of sentence structures used effectively, with accurate punctuation and spelling?

Refer to the examiner's mark scheme on page 107 and discuss with a partner what grade you think it might achieve. Highlight on the sample response where the assessment criteria are fulfilled.

## ◖ Over to you ...

Now answer the question yourself. Can you improve on the example?

Spend no more than 45 minutes on your answer. Remember to spend 5 minutes planning and sequencing your material before you begin writing, and 5 minutes checking your paragraphs, punctuation and spelling at the end.

GCSE English & Literature: Exam Preparation Support Pack © HarperCollins *Publishers* 2003

# Writing to advise

The writing to advise question in the exam requires you to show awareness of the following:

- The **purpose** of the writing – how well can you present your advice? Is it clear and easy to follow? Is it possible for the reader to find relevant information quickly and easily? Have you used devices such as headings, bullet points and underlining to help readers to navigate the text?
- The **audience** – how well suited to your audience is the advice given? Have you anticipated the needs and likely responses of your audience? Is the language used appropriate for the target audience?
- The **format** – are you aware of the conventions, such as headlines, bullet points or headings, of the kind of writing you have been given? How well do you use these conventions?

---

## Mock Question 3

A group of students at your school are planning an event to raise awareness of emotional health education. Prepare detailed **advice** on how best to do this.

You should include:

- the sort of event that will work well
- how to plan the event
- what targets to set
- how to follow up on the event's success.

---

## Planning and structuring your response

You should begin by identifying the audience, format and purpose of the task, and make some notes on what each aspect will require. Here are the notes made by one student:

> Audience - fellow students. Teenagers. Serious issue. Fairly formal style and language. Some homour?
>
> Format - Detailed instructions. Must be easy to follow - clear layout. Use bullet points and headings. Short paragraphs.
>
> Purpose - Instruction. Simple language. Clear structure.

Read through these notes with a partner. How might they be improved?

## Analysing a sample response

Sample Response 3 on page 109 is the start of an answer to the question. Read it and think about the following issues:

- Does it show an understanding of audience, format and purpose?
- Does it communicate clearly and imaginatively?
- Are the ideas organised well into sentences and paragraphs?
- Are a range of sentence structures used effectively, with accurate punctuation and spelling?

Refer to the examiner's mark scheme on page 107 and discuss with a partner what grade you think it might achieve. Highlight on the sample response where the assessment criteria are fulfilled.

## Over to you ...

Now answer the question yourself. Can you improve on the example?

Spend no more than 45 minutes on your answer. Remember to spend 5 minutes planning and sequencing your material before you begin writing, and 5 minutes checking your paragraphs, punctuation and spelling at the end.

GCSE English & Literature: Exam Preparation Support Pack © HarperCollins *Publishers* 2003

# Writing to inform

The writing to inform question in the exam requires you to show awareness of the following:

- The **purpose** of the writing – how well can you present your information? Can you present your ideas clearly in a way that readers can follow? Are you able to show which parts of the information are more or less important? How well can you use facts, figures, careful descriptions and accurate language to convey information clearly?
- The **audience** – is the information you present relevant to its audience? Is it expressed in appropriate language?
- The **format** – are you able to makes effective use of the conventions of this kind of writing, such as headings, bullet points or diagrams?

---

**Mock Question 4**

Almost everybody is an expert on something.

Write an **informative** article for your school magazine about one of your hobbies or interests.

---

## Planning and structuring your response

You should begin by identifying the audience, format and purpose of the task, and make some notes on what each aspect will require. Here are the notes made by one student:

> <u>Audience</u> - Known teenage audience. Informal style and language. 'I' point of view.
>
> <u>Format</u> - Article. Headline. Subheadings. Diagrams? Pictures sketches?
>
> <u>Purpose</u> - Inform. Start with what is interesting. Clearly structured account. Assume audience does not know about topic - explain things.

Read through these notes with a partner. How might they be improved?

## Analysing a sample response

Sample Response 4 on page 109 is the start of an answer to the question. Read it and think about the following issues:

- Does it show an understanding of audience, format and purpose?
- Does it communicate clearly and imaginatively?
- Are the ideas organised well into sentences and paragraphs?
- Are a range of sentence structures used effectively, with accurate punctuation and spelling?

Refer to the examiner's mark scheme on page 107 and discuss with a partner what grade you think it might achieve. Highlight on the sample response where the assessment criteria are fulfilled.

## Over to you ...

Now answer the question yourself, choosing one of your own hobbies or interests. Can you improve on the example?

Spend no more than 45 minutes on your answer. Remember to spend 5 minutes planning and sequencing your material before you begin writing, and 5 minutes checking your paragraphs, punctuation and spelling at the end.

# Writing to explain

The writing to explain question in the exam requires you to show awareness of the following:

- The **purpose** of the writing – how well can you present your explanation? Can you present ideas in a clear and logical way so that readers can follow? Are you able to use techniques such as facts, figures, descriptive language and precise details to make your explanation clear?
- The **audience** – is your argument presented in a way that will appeal to its target audience? Can you write using language appropriate for your audience?
- The **format** – are you aware of the conventions, such as headings, subheadings and bullet points, that are appropriate for the type of writing you have been given? Can you use these conventions effectively?

---

### Mock Question 5

Think of an event that changed your life in some way.

**Explain** what the event was and how it changed things for you.

---

## ◀ Planning and structuring your response

You should begin by identifying the audience, format and purpose of the task, and make some notes on what each aspect will require. Here are the notes made by one student:

> Audience – Not defined. Assume adult examiner and use formal style and language. 'I' point of view.
>
> Format – Not defined. Autobiographical writing. Remember to use paragraphs, vary sentence length and type.
>
> Purpose – Explain. Start with what happened. Move on to consequences. Good and bad things. Be clear about times things happened.

Read through these notes with a partner. How might they be improved?

## ◀ Analysing a sample response

Sample Response 5 on page 110 is the start of an answer to the question. Read it and think about the following issues:

- Does it show an understanding of audience, format and purpose?
- Does it communicate clearly and imaginatively?
- Are the ideas organised well into sentences and paragraphs?
- Are a range of sentence structures used effectively, with accurate punctuation and spelling?

Refer to the examiner's mark scheme on page 107 and discuss with a partner what grade you think it might achieve. Highlight on the sample response where the assessment criteria are fulfilled.

## ◀ Over to you ...

Now answer the question yourself, choosing your own important event. Can you improve on the example?

Spend no more than 45 minutes on your answer. Remember to spend 5 minutes planning and sequencing your material before you begin writing, and 5 minutes checking your paragraphs, punctuation and spelling at the end.

# Writing to describe

The writing to describe question in the exam requires you to show awareness of the following:

- The **purpose** of the writing – how well can you describe an event or a thing? Can you structure your description in an interesting way that is likely to engage the attention of your readers? Can you make your description engaging, using such things as metaphors and similes and other figures of speech? Can you convey a sense of a time, place or person accurately using a precise choice of words?
- The **audience** – is your description presented in a way that will appeal to its target audience? Is the language and style you have used appropriate for its audience?
- The **format** – are you aware of the conventions, such as headings and variations in paragraph and sentence length, that are appropriate to the kind of writing you have been given? How well do you use these conventions?

---

### Mock Question 6

**Describe** the room you are sitting in.

---

## ◀ Planning and structuring your response

You should begin by identifying the audience, format and purpose of the task, and make some notes on what each aspect will require. Here are the notes made by one student:

> <u>Audience</u> - Not defined. Assume adult examiner and use formal style and language. 'I' point of view.
>
> <u>Format</u> - Not defined. Autobiographical writing. Remember to use paragraphs, vary sentence length and type.
>
> <u>Purpose</u> - Describe. Use plenty of detail - help reader to imagine what is seen. Sense data - sights, sounds, smells etc. Some way of moving through the scene. Unusual approach.

Read through these notes with a partner. How might they be improved?

## ◀ Analysing a sample response

Sample Response 6 on page 110 is the start of an answer to the question. Read it and think about the following issues:

- Does it show an understanding of audience, format and purpose?
- Does it communicate clearly and imaginatively?
- Are the ideas organised well into sentences and paragraphs?
- Are a range of sentence structures used effectively, with accurate punctuation and spelling?

Refer to the examiner's mark scheme on page 107 and discuss with a partner what grade you think it might achieve. Highlight on the sample response where the assessment criteria are fulfilled.

## ◀ Over to you ...

Now answer the question yourself and describe your own classroom. Can you improve on the example?

Spend no more than 45 minutes on your answer. Remember to spend 5 minutes planning and sequencing your material before you begin writing, and 5 minutes checking your paragraphs, punctuation and spelling at the end.

# Examiner's mark scheme

The mark scheme below lists the assessment criteria that are used by examiners to grade the Writing sections of Papers 1 and 2.

## Skills

### 9–10 marks (notional Grade D)
- conscious attempt to suit the needs of purpose and audience and begins to engage reader's response
- clear, if mechanical, paragraphing, with more conscious use of vocabulary for effect
- some accurate spelling of more complex words, and uses a range of punctuation

### 11–12 marks (notional Grade C)
- clear identification with purpose and audience; begins to sustain reader's response
- evidence of structure with usually coherent paragraphs and clear selection of vocabulary for effect
- generally secure in spelling and in punctuation which clarifies meaning and purpose

### 13–14 marks (notional Grade B)
- form, content and style are generally matched to purpose and audience
- well structured, starting to use paragraphs to enhance meaning and with increasing sophistication in vocabulary choice
- generally secure in spelling and in punctuation which clarifies meaning and purpose

### 15–16 marks (notional Grade A)
- form, content and style are consistently matched to purpose and audience
- coherently structured with fluently linked sentence structures and paragraphs and evidence of conscious crafting
- achieves a high level of technical accuracy in spelling and punctuation

### 17–18 marks (notional Grade A*)
- form, content and style are assuredly matched to purpose and audience; distinctive and consistently effective
- controlled and sustained crafting with highly effective and delightful vocabulary choices
- achieves a high level of technical accuracy in spelling and punctuation

There are three Assessment Objectives for this part of the exam (see below).

Candidates are required to demonstrate their ability to:
- communicate clearly and imaginatively, using and adapting forms for different readers and purposes;
- organise ideas into sentences, paragraphs and whole texts using a variety of linguistic and structural features;
- use a range of sentence structures effectively with accurate punctuation and spelling.

GCSE English & Literature: Exam Preparation Support Pack © HarperCollins *Publishers* 2003

### Sample Response 1

## It's good to talk

Remember that old BT slogan? Well it's mostly true. Talking is good for you if it's the right kind of talk. Some people talk all day but they never actually say anything important. Other people hardly say a word. Both groups need to think about talking about what matters to them. If you don't learn to share your feelings you may never have a successful relationship or be building up psychological problems for yourself.

My big dictionary tells me that talking all day and not actually saying anything is called phatic communication. It is about being sociable and friendly rather than passing on messages or important information. My mum is very good at this sort of talk and my dad is useless at it. In fact, my mum can do both sides of a conversation at once if you don't answer her quickly enough. Dad can talk for hours about car engines or football but he tends to get really stumped by simple questions like 'How are you?'

### Sample Response 2

You might ask why we need a counselling service when the building is already full of people students can talk to. Apart from class and form teachers there are Heads of Year and their assistants, the senior staff, even some of the caretaking staff are quite friendly. As well as these people there are parents at home and of course over 900 students to choose from. Why do we need a counsellor?

The answer is that often when you have problems you don't want to talk to the people you normally deal with. Your friend might also be friends with the person causing the problem. You might worry that your teacher will treat you differently in class, your parents may be causing your stress in the first place. A trained counsellor will work in the school, but he or she will be outside the normal system. Students will have a sympathetic ear in school that they can go to and not worry about meeting in a lesson half an hour later.

Sometimes just talking about a problem can solve it. It is very easy to get obsessed by coping with coursework deadlines or the fact that you don't have any real friends. Such ideas go round and round in your head so that you end up not doing any coursework because you spend all your time worrying about it, or your friends become less friendly because they can see you don't trust them. Teachers know their own areas but they are not often aware of the bigger picture, and friends might not take kindly to being asked if they are real. A counsellor would be able to listen to these and all sorts of other problems without being directly involved.

GCSE English & Literature: Exam Preparation Support Pack © HarperCollins *Publishers* 2003

## Sample Response 3

<u>Choosing your event</u>

In choosing your event there are two major possibilities:

· A publicity event
· An awareness raising event

Publicity events are things like sponsored walks or balloon races. They get your topic into everybody's minds but they don't actually involve anything to do with improving emotional health education. Publicity events are best used at the start of a project to get people talking and thinking or, if necessary, to raise money.

Awareness raising events are things like conferences, workshops or invited speakers. They actually involve improving emotional health education in the event itself so that people should go away from them feeling that they have learned something. If no one in your school has any idea at all what emotional health education is an awareness raising event is probably the best place to start.

## Sample Response 4

I have been interested in black and white photography for several years now and I have always found it a fascinating and rewarding pastime. I suppose this kind of photography is quite old fashioned now that everyone has got digital cameras and can manipulate images on computers but I find its still a lot of fun. There are three main parts to my hobby: choosing an image; setting the camera and developing and printing. I will deal with each aspect in turn.

<u>Choosing an image.</u>
One of the things I like about working in black and white is that you are not distracted by all the colours in a scene. Instead you have to concentrate on things like shape, composition and texture as well as all the usual stuff about light, exposure and depth of field. I realise I have just used a bunch of technical terms, but don't worry, I'll explain each one as we go along. Shape, for instance, means what it says but when you are working in black and white you have to remember that colour boundaries will not necessarily be obvious when they have been reduced to shades of grey. Sometimes scenes that look great to the naked eye are disappointing in the photograph, but sometimes the black and white image shows you things that you would hardly even notice on an everyday basis.

GCSE English & Literature: Exam Preparation Support Pack © HarperCollins *Publishers* 2003

# Sample responses 5–6

## Sample Response 5

The event that changed my life the most (so far) is moving to a new school five years ago. I can't remember if I was looking forward to secondary school or dreading it but, as it turned out, I should have been dreading it.

I enjoyed my time in primary school and I was quite good in most subjects. Most of my friends were planning to come to the same secondary school as me so I suppose I thought that the new school wouldn't be too much of a problem. At first this was true. We had the usual period of meeting new people, getting lost on our way to lessons and having to listen to Year 11s saying, 'Aren't they small!'. I was put in a tutor group with three people from my old class and obviously I saw my old friends at break and dinner time.

The trouble started just after Christmas in the first year. I remember it was a fairly ordinary winter's day, there was the usual vicious wind blasting between the science block and the Gym, and my friends and I were wandering around looking for somewhere to shelter. We saw a new Year 7 student in one of our favourite places and, being a friendly group, we went over to talk to him. Even now, five years later, I still think about that break time. What if it had been raining and we'd stayed inside? Or what if we'd decided to queue for some food instead of going out? But neither of these things happened and we went over to talk to the boy.

## Sample Response 6

Well here we are at the annual student torture festival known as the GCSE exams. Last time I was in this room, for the mock exams, it was freezing cold. Now it's boiling hot. Last time it was like a scene from "A Christmas Carol", with students wearing those gloves without fingers and rubbing their hands to keep them warm. This time it's like a scene from "Bridge over the River Kwai" with sweat breaking out on the backs of everybody's shirts and cruel guards patrolling around to make sure no one escapes.

Of course, its not exactly like a Japanese prisoner of war camp in here. You tended to get better views in POW camps for one thing. Our school hall, where I sit with 150 other unfortunates, seems to have been designed by someone who thought that the ability to look out the window might distract pupils from their head teacher's words of wisdom so the whole thing is designed like a box. Light comes in from somewhere but the rumour that there are windows near the top has never been proved; the last expedition to find them was lost in an ill-advised attempt to scale the stage curtains. Electric light is provided by things that would look like flying saucers if it weren't for the power cables holding them up.

You'd think that a virtually windowless box would be cool in the summer but the genius who designed it forgot to include cavity wall insulation and so we all sit here sweltering whilst somewhere outside birds sing and there are still some little children who haven't heard of GCSEs. Inside everyone wishes they hadn't heard of them either.

GCSE English & Literature: Exam Preparation Support Pack © HarperCollins *Publishers* 2003